MW00466129

On
High
Performance

HBR's 10 Must Reads series is the definitive collection of ideas and best practices for aspiring and experienced leaders alike. These books offer essential reading selected from the pages of *Harvard Business Review* on topics critical to the success of every manager.

Titles include:

HBR's 10 Must Reads 2015
HBR's 10 Must Reads 2016
HBR's 10 Must Reads 2017
HBR's 10 Must Reads 2018
HBR's 10 Must Reads 2019
HBR's 10 Must Reads 2020
HBR's 10 Must Reads 2021
HBR's 10 Must Reads 2022
HBR's 10 Must Reads for CEOs
HBR's 10 Must Reads for New Managers
HBR's 10 Must Reads on AI, Analytics, and the New Machine Age
HBR's 10 Must Reads on Boards
HBR's 10 Must Reads on Building a Great Culture
HBR's 10 Must Reads on Business Model Innovation
HBR's 10 Must Reads on Career Resilience
HBR's 10 Must Reads on Change Management (Volumes 1 and 2)
HBR's 10 Must Reads on Collaboration
HBR's 10 Must Reads on Communication (Volumes 1 and 2)
HBR's 10 Must Reads on Creativity
HBR's 10 Must Reads on Design Thinking
HBR's 10 Must Reads on Diversity
HBR's 10 Must Reads on Emotional Intelligence
HBR's 10 Must Reads on Entrepreneurship and Startups
HBR's 10 Must Reads on High Performance
HBR's 10 Must Reads on Innovation
HBR's 10 Must Reads on Leadership (Volumes 1 and 2)
HBR's 10 Must Reads on Leadership for Healthcare

On
High
Performance

HARVARD BUSINESS REVIEW PRESS
Boston, Massachusetts

Copyright 2022 Harvard Business School Publishing Corporation
All rights reserved
Printed in the United States of America
5 2023

Library of Congress Cataloging-in-Publication Data

Title: HBR's 10 must reads on high performance.
Other titles: Harvard Business Review's ten must reads on high performance |
    HBR's 10 must reads (Series)
Description: Boston, Massachusetts : Harvard Business Review Press, [2022] |
    Series: HBR's 10 must reads | Includes index.
Identifiers: LCCN 2021057332 (print) | LCCN 2021057333 (ebook) |
    ISBN 9781647823467 (paperback) | ISBN 9781647823474 (epub)
Subjects: LCSH: Work—Psychological aspects. | Performance. |
    Success in business.
Classification: LCC BF481 .H397 2022 (print) | LCC BF481 (ebook) |
    DDC 158.7—dc23/eng/20220103
LC record available at https://lccn.loc.gov/2021057332
LC ebook record available at https://lccn.loc.gov/2021057333

ISBN: 978-1-64782-346-7
eISBN: 978-1-64782-347-4

Contents

On
High
Performance

The Making of an Expert

by K. Anders Ericsson, Michael J. Prietula, and Edward T. Cokely

THIRTY YEARS AGO, two Hungarian educators, László and Klara Polgár, decided to challenge the popular assumption that women don't succeed in areas requiring spatial thinking, such as chess. They wanted to make a point about the power of education. The Polgárs homeschooled their three daughters, and as part of their education the girls started playing chess with their parents at a very young age. Their systematic training and daily practice paid off. By 2000, all three daughters had been ranked in the top ten female players in the world. The youngest, Judit, had become a grand master at age 15, breaking the previous record for the youngest person to earn that title, held by Bobby Fischer, by a month.

Today Judit is one of the world's top players and has defeated almost all the best male players.

It's not only assumptions about gender differences in expertise that have started to crumble. Back in 1985, Benjamin Bloom, a professor of education at the University of Chicago, published a landmark book, *Developing Talent in Young People,* which examined the critical factors that contribute to talent. He took a deep retrospective look at the childhoods of 120 elite performers who had won international competitions or awards in fields ranging from music and the arts to mathematics and neurology. Surprisingly, Bloom's work found no early indicators that could have predicted the virtuosos' success. Subsequent research indicating that there is no correlation between IQ and expert performance in fields such as chess, music, sports, and medicine has borne out his findings. The only innate differences that turn out to be significant—and they matter primarily in sports—are height and body size.

So what *does* correlate with success? One thing emerges very clearly from Bloom's work: All the superb performers he investigated had practiced intensively, had studied with devoted teachers, and had been supported enthusiastically by their families throughout their developing years. Later research building on Bloom's pioneering study revealed that the amount and quality of practice were key factors in the level of expertise people achieved. Consistently and overwhelmingly, the evidence showed that *experts are always made, not born.* These conclusions are based on rigorous research that looked at exceptional performance using scientific methods that are verifiable and reproducible. Most of these studies were compiled in *The Cambridge Handbook of Expertise and Expert Performance,* published last year by Cambridge University Press and edited by K. Anders Ericsson, one of the authors of this article. The 900-page-plus handbook includes contributions from more than 100 leading scientists who have studied expertise and top performance in a wide variety of domains: surgery, acting, chess, writing, computer programming, ballet, music, aviation, firefighting, and many others.

The journey to truly superior performance is neither for the faint of heart nor for the impatient. The development of genuine expertise requires struggle, sacrifice, and honest, often painful self-assessment. There are no shortcuts. It will take you at least a decade to achieve expertise, and you will need to invest that time wisely, by engaging in "deliberate" practice—practice that focuses on tasks beyond your current level of competence and comfort. You will need a well-informed coach not only to guide you through deliberate practice but also to help you learn how to coach yourself. Above all, if you want to achieve top performance as a manager and a leader, you've got to forget the folklore about genius that makes many people think they cannot take a scientific approach to developing expertise. We are here to help you explode those myths.

Let's begin our story with a little wine.

What Is an Expert?

In 1976, a fascinating event referred to as the "Judgment of Paris" took place. An English-owned wineshop in Paris organized a blind tasting in which nine French wine experts rated French and California wines—ten whites and ten reds. The results shocked the wine world: California wines received the highest scores from the panel. Even more surprising, during the tasting the experts often mistook the American wines for French wines and vice versa.

Two assumptions were challenged that day. The first was the hitherto unquestioned superiority of French wines over American ones. But it was the challenge to the second—the assumption that the judges genuinely possessed elite knowledge of wine—that was more interesting and revolutionary. The tasting suggested that the alleged wine experts were no more accurate in distinguishing wines under blind test conditions than regular wine drinkers—a fact later confirmed by our laboratory tests.

Current research has revealed many other fields where there is no scientific evidence that supposed expertise leads to superior performance. One study showed that psychotherapists with advanced degrees and decades of experience aren't reliably more successful in their treatment of randomly assigned patients than novice therapists with just three months of training are. There are even examples of expertise seeming to decline with experience. The longer physicians have been out of training, for example, the less able they are to identify unusual diseases of the lungs or heart. Because they encounter these illnesses so rarely, doctors quickly forget their characteristic features and have difficulty diagnosing them. Performance picks up only after the doctors undergo a refresher course.

How, then, can you tell when you're dealing with a genuine expert? Real expertise must pass three tests. First, it must lead to

Things to Look Out for When
Judging Expertise

Individual accounts of expertise are often unreliable.

Anecdotes, selective recall, and one-off events all can present insufficient, often misleading, examples of expertise. There is a huge body of literature on false memories, self-serving biases, and recollections altered as a result of current beliefs or the passage of time. Reporting is not the same thing as research.

Many people are wrongly believed to possess expertise.

Bear in mind that true expertise is demonstrated by measurable, consistently superior performance. Some supposed experts are superior only when it comes to explaining why they made errors. After the 1976 Judgment of Paris, for example, when California wines bested French wines in a blind tasting, the French wine "experts" argued that the results were an aberration and that the California reds in particular would never age as well as the famous French reds. (In 2006, the tasting of the reds was reenacted, and California came out on top again.) Had it not been for the objective results from the blind tastings, the French wine experts may never have been convinced of the quality of the American wines.

Intuition can lead you down the garden path.

The idea that you can improve your performance by relaxing and "just trusting your gut" is popular. While it may be true that intuition is valuable

---

performance that is consistently superior to that of the expert's peers. Second, real expertise produces concrete results. Brain surgeons, for example, not only must be skillful with their scalpels but also must have successful outcomes with their patients. A chess player must be able to win matches in tournaments. Finally, true expertise can be replicated and measured in the lab. As the British scientist Lord Kelvin stated, "If you can not measure it, you can not improve it."

Skill in some fields, such as sports, is easy to measure. Competitions are standardized so that everyone competes in a similar environment. All competitors have the same start and finish lines, so that everyone can agree on who came in first. That standardiza-

in routine or familiar situations, informed intuition is the result of deliberate practice. You cannot consistently improve your ability to make decisions (or your intuition) without considerable practice, reflection, and analysis.

You don't need a different putter.

Many managers hope that they will suddenly improve performance by adopting new and better methods—just as golf players may think that they can lower their scores with a new and better club. But changing to a different putter may increase the variability of a golfer's shot and thus hinder his or her ability to play well. In reality, the key to improving expertise is consistency and carefully controlled efforts.

Expertise is not captured by knowledge management systems.

Knowledge management systems rarely, if ever, deal with what psychologists call knowledge. They are repositories of images, documents, and routines: external data that people can view and interpret as they try to solve a problem or make a decision. There are no shortcuts to gaining true expertise.

tion permits comparisons among individuals over time, and it's certainly possible in business as well. In the early days of Walmart, for instance, Sam Walton arranged competitions among store managers to identify those whose stores had the highest profitability. Each store in the Nordstrom clothing chain posts rankings of its salespeople, based on their sales per hour, for each pay period.

Nonetheless, it often can be difficult to measure expert performance—for example, in projects that take months or even years to complete and to which dozens of individuals may contribute. Expert leadership is similarly difficult to assess. Most leadership challenges are highly complex and specific to a given company, which makes it hard to compare performance across companies and situations. That doesn't mean, though, that scientists should throw up their hands and stop trying to measure performance. One methodology we use to deal with these challenges is to take a representative situation and reproduce it in the laboratory. For example, we present emergency room nurses with scenarios that simulate life-threatening situations. Afterward, we compare the nurses' responses in the lab with actual outcomes in the real world. We have found that performance in simulations in medicine, chess, and sports closely correlates with objective measurements of expert performance, such as a chess player's track record in winning matches.

Testing methodologies can be devised for creative professions such as art and writing, too. Researchers have studied differences among individual visual artists, for instance, by having them produce drawings of the same set of objects. With the artists' identities concealed, these drawings were evaluated by art judges, whose ratings clearly agreed on the artists' proficiency, especially in regard to technical aspects of drawing. Other researchers have designed objective tasks to measure the superior perceptual skills of artists without the help of judges.

Practice Deliberately

To people who have never reached a national or international level of competition, it may appear that excellence is simply the result of practicing daily for years or even decades. However, living in a cave does not make you a geologist. Not all practice makes perfect. You need a particular kind of practice—*deliberate practice*—to develop expertise. When most people practice, they focus on the things they already know how to do. Deliberate practice is different. It entails considerable, specific, and sustained efforts to do something you *can't* do well—or even at all. Research across domains shows that it is only by working at what you can't do that you turn into the expert you want to become.

To illustrate this point, let's imagine you are learning to play golf for the first time. In the early phases, you try to understand the basic strokes and focus on avoiding gross mistakes (like driving the ball into another player). You practice on the putting green, hit balls at a driving range, and play rounds with others who are most likely novices like you. In a surprisingly short time (perhaps 50 hours), you will develop better control and your game will improve. From then on, you will work on your skills by driving and putting more balls and engaging in more games, until your strokes become automatic: You'll think less about each shot and play more from intuition. Your golf game now is a social outing, in which you occasionally concentrate on your shot. From this point on, additional time on the course will not substantially improve your performance, which may remain at the same level for decades.

Why does this happen? You don't improve because when you are playing a game, you get only a single chance to make a shot from any given location. You don't get to figure out how you can correct mistakes. If you were allowed to take five to ten shots from the exact same location on the course, you would get more feedback on your technique and start to adjust your playing style to improve your control. In fact, professionals often take multiple shots from the same location when they train and when they check out a course before a tournament.

This kind of deliberate practice can be adapted to developing business and leadership expertise. The classic example is the case method taught by many business schools, which presents students with real-life situations that require action. Because the eventual outcomes of those situations are known, the students can immediately judge the merits of their proposed solutions. In this way, they can practice making decisions ten to 20 times a week. War games serve a similar training function at military academies. Officers can analyze the trainees' responses in simulated combat and provide an instant evaluation. Such mock military operations sharpen leadership skills with deliberate practice that lets trainees explore uncharted areas.

Let's take a closer look at how deliberate practice might work for leadership. You often hear that a key element of leadership and management is charisma, which is true. Being a leader frequently requires standing in front of your employees, your peers, or your board of directors and attempting to convince them of one thing or another, especially in times of crisis. A surprising number of executives believe that charisma is innate and cannot be learned. Yet if they were acting in a play with the help of a director and a coach, most of them would be able to come across as considerably more charismatic, especially over time. In fact, working with a leading drama school, we have developed a set of acting exercises for managers and leaders that are designed to increase their powers of charm and persuasion. Executives who do these exercises have shown remarkable improvement. So charisma can be learned through deliberate practice. Bear in mind that even Winston Churchill, one of the most charismatic figures of the twentieth century, practiced his oratory style in front of a mirror.

Genuine experts not only practice deliberately but also *think* deliberately. The golfer Ben Hogan once explained, "While I am practicing I am also trying to develop my powers of concentration. I never just walk up and hit the ball." Hogan would decide in advance where he wanted the ball to go and how to get it there. We actually track this kind of thought process in our research. We present expert performers with a scenario and ask them to think aloud as they work their way through it. Chess players, for example, will describe how they spend five to ten minutes exploring all the possibilities for their next move, thinking through the consequences of each and planning out the sequence of moves that might follow it. We've observed that when a course of action doesn't work out as expected, the expert players will go back to their prior analysis to assess where they went wrong and how to avoid future errors. They continually work to eliminate their weaknesses.

Deliberate practice involves two kinds of learning: improving the skills you already have and extending the reach and range of your skills. The enormous concentration required to undertake these twin tasks limits the amount of time you can spend doing them. The famous violinist Nathan Milstein wrote: "Practice as much as you feel you can accomplish with concentration. Once when I became concerned because others around me practiced all day long, I asked [my mentor] Professor Auer how many hours I should practice, and he said, 'It really doesn't matter how long. If you practice with your fingers, no amount is enough. If you practice with your head, two hours is plenty.'"

It is interesting to note that across a wide range of experts, including athletes, novelists, and musicians, very few appear to be able to engage in more than four or five hours of high concentration and deliberate practice at a time. In fact, most expert teachers and scientists set aside only a couple of hours a day, typically in the morning, for their most demanding mental activities, such as writing about new ideas. While this may seem like a relatively small investment, it is two hours a day more than most executives and managers devote to building their skills, since the majority of their time is consumed by meetings and day-to-day concerns. This difference adds up to some 700 hours more a year, or about 7,000 hours more a decade. Think about what you could accomplish if you devoted two hours a day to deliberate practice.

It's very easy to neglect deliberate practice. Experts who reach a high level of performance often find themselves responding automatically to specific situations and may come to rely exclusively on their intuition. This leads to difficulties when they deal with atypical or rare cases, because they've lost the ability to analyze a situation and work through the right response. Experts may not recognize this creeping intuition bias, of course, because there is no penalty until they encounter a situation in which a habitual response fails and maybe even causes damage. Older professionals with a great deal of experience are particularly prone to falling into this trap, but it's certainly not inevitable. Research has shown that musicians over 60 years old who continue deliberate practice for about ten hours a week can match the speed and technical skills of 20-year-old expert musicians when tested on their ability to play a piece of unfamiliar music.

Moving outside your traditional comfort zone of achievement requires substantial motivation and sacrifice, but it's a necessary discipline. As the golf champion Sam Snead once put it, "It is only human nature to want to practice what you can already do well, since it's a hell of a lot less work and a hell of a lot more fun." Only when you can see that deliberate practice is the most effective means to the desired end—becoming the best in your field—will you commit to excellence. Snead, who died in 2002, held the record for winning the most PGA Tour events and was famous for having one of the most beautiful swings in the sport. Deliberate practice was a key to his success. "Practice puts brains in your muscles," he said.

Take the Time You Need

By now it will be clear that it takes time to become an expert. Our research shows that even the most gifted performers need a minimum of ten years (or 10,000 hours) of intense training before they win international competitions. In some fields the apprenticeship is longer: It now takes most elite musicians 15 to 25 years of steady practice, on average, before they succeed at the international level.

Though there are historical examples of people who attained an international level of expertise at an early age, it's also true that, in the nineteenth and early twentieth centuries, people could reach world-class levels more quickly. In most fields, the bar of performance has risen steadily since that time. For instance, amateur marathon runners and high school swimmers today frequently better the times of Olympic gold medalists from the early twentieth century. Increasingly stiff competition now makes it almost impossible to beat the ten-year rule. One notable exception, Bobby Fischer, did manage to become a chess grand master in just nine years, but it is likely that he did so by spending more time practicing each year.

Many people are naive about how long it takes to become an expert. Leo Tolstoy once observed that people often told him they didn't know whether or not they could write a novel because they hadn't tried—as if they only had to make a single attempt to discover their natural ability to write. Similarly, the authors of many self-help books appear to assume that their readers are essentially ready for success and simply need to take a few more easy steps to overcome great hurdles. Popular lore is full of stories about unknown athletes, writers, and artists who become famous overnight, seemingly because of innate talent—they're "naturals," people say. However, when examining the developmental histories of experts, we unfailingly discover that they spent a lot of time in training and preparation. Sam Snead, who'd been called "the best natural player ever," told *Golf Digest,* "People always said I had a natural swing. They thought I wasn't a hard worker. But when I was young, I'd play and practice all day, then practice more at night by my car's headlights. My hands bled. Nobody worked harder at golf than I did."

Not only do you have to be prepared to invest time in becoming an expert, but you have to start early—at least in some fields. Your ability to attain expert performance is clearly constrained if you have fewer opportunities to engage in deliberate practice, and this is far from a trivial constraint. Once, after giving a talk, K. Anders Ericsson was asked by a member of the audience whether he or any other person could win an Olympic medal if he began training at a mature age. Nowadays, Ericsson replied, it would be virtually impossible for anyone to win an individual medal without a training history comparable with that of today's elite performers, nearly all of whom started very early. Many children simply do not get the opportunity, for whatever reason, to work with the best teachers and to engage in the sort of deliberate practice that they need to reach the Olympic level in a sport.

Find Coaches and Mentors

Arguably the most famous violin teacher of all time, Ivan Galamian, made the point that budding maestros do not engage in deliberate practice spontaneously: "If we analyze the development of the well-known artists, we see that in almost every case the success of their entire career was dependent on the quality of their practicing. In practically every case, the practicing was constantly supervised either by the teacher or an assistant to the teacher."

Research on world-class performers has confirmed Galamian's observation. It also has shown that future experts need different kinds of teachers at different stages of their development. In the beginning, most are coached by local teachers, people who can give generously of their time and praise. Later on, however, it is essential that performers seek out more-advanced teachers to keep improving their skills. Eventually, all top performers work closely with teachers who have themselves reached international levels of achievement.

Having expert coaches makes a difference in a variety of ways. To start with, they can help you accelerate your learning process. The thirteenth-century philosopher and scientist Roger Bacon argued that it would be impossible to master mathematics in less than 30 years. And yet today individuals can master frameworks as complex as calculus in their teens. The difference is that scholars have since organized the material in such a way that it is much more accessible. Students of mathematics no longer have to climb Everest by themselves; they can follow a guide up a well-trodden path.

The development of expertise requires coaches who are capable of giving constructive, even painful, feedback. Real experts are extremely motivated students who seek out such feedback. They're also skilled at understanding when and if a coach's advice doesn't work for them. The elite performers we studied knew what they were doing right and concentrated on what they were doing wrong. They deliberately picked unsentimental coaches who would challenge them and drive them to higher levels of performance. The best coaches also identify aspects of your performance that will need to be improved at your *next* level of skill. If a coach pushes you too fast, too hard, you will only be frustrated and may even be tempted to give up trying to improve at all.

Relying on a coach has its limits, however. Statistics show that radiologists correctly diagnose breast cancer from X-rays about 70% of the time. Typically, young radiologists learn the skill of interpreting X-rays by working alongside an "expert." So it's hardly surprising that the success rate has stuck at 70% for a long time. Imagine how much better radiology might get if radiologists practiced instead by making diagnostic judgments using X-rays in a library of old verified cases, where they could immediately determine their accuracy. We're seeing these kinds of techniques used more often in training. There is an emerging market in elaborate simulations that can give professionals, especially in medicine and aviation, a safe way to deliberately practice with appropriate feedback.

So what happens when you become an Olympic gold medalist, or an international chess master, or a CEO? Ideally, as your expertise increased, your coach will have helped you become more and more independent, so that you are able to set your own development plans. Like good parents who encourage their children to leave the nest, good coaches help their students learn how to rely on an "inner coach." Self-coaching can be done in any field. Expert surgeons, for example, are not concerned with a patient's postoperative status alone. They will study any unanticipated events that took place during the surgery, to try to figure out how mistakes or misjudgments can be avoided in the future.

Benjamin Franklin provides one of the best examples of motivated self-coaching. When he wanted to learn to write eloquently and persuasively, he began to study his favorite articles from a popular British publication, the *Spectator*. Days after he'd read an article he particularly enjoyed, he would try to reconstruct it from memory in his own words. Then he would compare it with the original, so he could discover and correct his faults. He also worked to improve his sense of language by translating the articles into rhyming verse and then from verse back into prose. Similarly, famous painters sometimes attempt to reproduce the paintings of other masters.

Anyone can apply these same methods on the job. Say you have someone in your company who is a masterly communicator, and you learn that he is going to give a talk to a unit that will be laying off workers. Sit down and write your own speech, and then compare his actual speech with what you wrote. Observe the reactions to his talk and imagine what the reactions would be to yours. Each time you can generate by yourself decisions, interactions, or speeches that match those of people who excel, you move one step closer to reaching the level of an expert performer.

Before practice, opportunity, and luck can combine to create expertise, the would-be expert needs to demythologize the achievement of top-level performance, because the notion that genius is born, not made, is deeply ingrained. It's perhaps most perfectly exemplified in the person of Wolfgang Amadeus Mozart, who is typically presented as a child prodigy with exceptional innate musical genius. Nobody questions that Mozart's achievements were extraordinary compared with those of his contemporaries. What's often forgotten, however, is that his development was equally exceptional for his time. His musical tutelage started before he was four years old, and his father, also a skilled composer, was a famous music teacher and had written one of the first books on violin instruction. Like other world-class performers, Mozart was not born an expert—he became one.

Originally published July–August 2007. Reprint R0707J

Managing Oneself

by Peter F. Drucker

HISTORY'S GREAT ACHIEVERS—a Napoléon, a da Vinci, a Mozart—
have always managed themselves. That, in large measure, is what
makes them great achievers. But they are rare exceptions, so unusual
both in their talents and their accomplishments as to be considered
outside the boundaries of ordinary human existence. Now, most of
us, even those of us with modest endowments, will have to learn to
manage ourselves. We will have to learn to develop ourselves. We
will have to place ourselves where we can make the greatest contribution. And we will have to stay mentally alert and engaged during
a 50-year working life, which means knowing how and when to
change the work we do.

What Are My Strengths?

Most people think they know what they are good at. They are usually wrong. More often, people know what they are not good at—
and even then more people are wrong than right. And yet, a person
can perform only from strength. One cannot build performance on
weaknesses, let alone on something one cannot do at all.

Throughout history, people had little need to know their strengths.
A person was born into a position and a line of work: The peasant's son
would also be a peasant; the artisan's daughter, an artisan's wife; and

so on. But now people have choices. We need to know our strengths in order to know where we belong.

The only way to discover your strengths is through feedback analysis. Whenever you make a key decision or take a key action, write down what you expect will happen. Nine or 12 months later, compare the actual results with your expectations. I have been practicing this method for 15 to 20 years now, and every time I do it, I am surprised. The feedback analysis showed me, for instance—and to my great surprise—that I have an intuitive understanding of technical people, whether they are engineers or accountants or market researchers. It also showed me that I don't really resonate with generalists.

Feedback analysis is by no means new. It was invented sometime in the fourteenth century by an otherwise totally obscure German theologian and picked up quite independently, some 150 years later, by John Calvin and Ignatius of Loyola, each of whom incorporated it into the practice of his followers. In fact, the steadfast focus on performance and results that this habit produces explains why the institutions these two men founded, the Calvinist church and the Jesuit order, came to dominate Europe within 30 years.

Practiced consistently, this simple method will show you within a fairly short period of time, maybe two or three years, where your strengths lie—and this is the most important thing to know. The method will show you what you are doing or failing to do that deprives you of the full benefits of your strengths. It will show you where you are not particularly competent. And finally, it will show you where you have no strengths and cannot perform.

Several implications for action follow from feedback analysis. First and foremost, concentrate on your strengths. Put yourself where your strengths can produce results.

Second, work on improving your strengths. Analysis will rapidly show where you need to improve skills or acquire new ones. It will also show the gaps in your knowledge—and those can usually be filled. Mathematicians are born, but everyone can learn trigonometry.

Third, discover where your intellectual arrogance is causing disabling ignorance and overcome it. Far too many people—especially

Idea in Brief

We live in an age of unprecedented opportunity: If you've got ambition, drive, and smarts, you can rise to the top of your chosen profession—regardless of where you started out. But with opportunity comes responsibility. Companies today aren't managing their knowledge workers' careers. Rather, we must each be our own chief executive officer.

Simply put, it's up to you to carve out your place in the work world and know when to change course. And it's up to you to keep yourself engaged and productive during a work life that may span some 50 years.

To do all of these things well, you'll need to cultivate a deep understanding of yourself. What are your most valuable strengths and most dangerous weaknesses? Equally important, how do you learn and work with others? What are your most deeply held values? And in what type of work environment can you make the greatest contribution?

The implication is clear: Only when you operate from a combination of your strengths and self-knowledge can you achieve true—and lasting—excellence.

people with great expertise in one area—are contemptuous of knowledge in other areas or believe that being bright is a substitute for knowledge. First-rate engineers, for instance, tend to take pride in not knowing anything about people. Human beings, they believe, are much too disorderly for the good engineering mind. Human resources professionals, by contrast, often pride themselves on their ignorance of elementary accounting or of quantitative methods altogether. But taking pride in such ignorance is self-defeating. Go to work on acquiring the skills and knowledge you need to fully realize your strengths.

It is equally essential to remedy your bad habits—the things you do or fail to do that inhibit your effectiveness and performance. Such habits will quickly show up in the feedback. For example, a planner may find that his beautiful plans fail because he does not follow through on them. Like so many brilliant people, he believes that ideas move mountains. But bulldozers move mountains; ideas show where the bulldozers should go to work. This planner will have to learn that the work does not stop when the plan is completed. He

Idea in Practice

To build a life of excellence, begin by asking yourself these questions:

"What are my strengths?"

To accurately identify your strengths, use **feedback analysis**. Every time you make a key decision, write down the outcome you expect. Several months later, compare the actual results with your expected results. Look for patterns in what you're seeing: What results are you skilled at generating? What abilities do you need to enhance in order to get the results you want? What unproductive habits are preventing you from creating the outcomes you desire? In identifying opportunities for improvement, don't waste time cultivating skill areas where you have little competence. Instead, concentrate on—and build on—your strengths.

"How do I work?"

In what ways do you work best? Do you process information most effectively by reading it, or by hearing others discuss it? Do you accomplish the most by working with other people, or by working alone? Do you perform best while making decisions, or while advising others on key matters? Are you in top form when things get stressful, or do you function optimally in a highly predictable environment?

"What are my values?"

What are your ethics? What do you see as your most important responsibilities for living a worthy, ethical life? Do your organization's ethics resonate with your own values? If not, your career will likely be marked by frustration and poor performance.

"Where do I belong?"

Consider your strengths, preferred work style, and values. Based on these qualities, in what kind of work environment would you fit in best? Find the perfect fit, and you'll transform yourself from a merely acceptable employee into a star performer.

"What can I contribute?"

In earlier eras, companies told businesspeople what their contribution should be. Today, you have choices. To decide how you can best enhance your organization's performance, first ask what the situation requires. Based on your strengths, work style, and values, how might you make the greatest contribution to your organization's efforts?

must find people to carry out the plan and explain it to them. He must adapt and change it as he puts it into action. And finally, he must decide when to stop pushing the plan.

At the same time, feedback will also reveal when the problem is a lack of manners. Manners are the lubricating oil of an organization. It is a law of nature that two moving bodies in contact with each other create friction. This is as true for human beings as it is for inanimate objects. Manners—simple things like saying "please" and "thank you" and knowing a person's name or asking after her family—enable two people to work together whether they like each other or not. Bright people, especially bright young people, often do not understand this. If analysis shows that someone's brilliant work fails again and again as soon as cooperation from others is required, it probably indicates a lack of courtesy—that is, a lack of manners.

Comparing your expectations with your results also indicates what not to do. We all have a vast number of areas in which we have no talent or skill and little chance of becoming even mediocre. In those areas a person—and especially a knowledge worker—should not take on work, jobs, and assignments. One should waste as little effort as possible on improving areas of low competence. It takes far more energy and work to improve from incompetence to mediocrity than it takes to improve from first-rate performance to excellence. And yet most people—especially most teachers and most organizations—concentrate on making incompetent performers into mediocre ones. Energy, resources, and time should go instead to making a competent person into a star performer.

How Do I Perform?

Amazingly few people know how they get things done. Indeed, most of us do not even know that different people work and perform differently. Too many people work in ways that are not their ways, and that almost guarantees nonperformance. For knowledge workers, How do I perform? may be an even more important question than What are my strengths?

Like one's strengths, how one performs is unique. It is a matter of personality. Whether personality be a matter of nature or nurture, it surely is formed long before a person goes to work. And *how* a person performs is a given, just as *what* a person is good at or not good at is a given. A person's way of performing can be slightly modified, but it is unlikely to be completely changed—and certainly not easily. Just as people achieve results by doing what they are good at, they also achieve results by working in ways that they best perform. A few common personality traits usually determine how a person performs.

Am I a reader or a listener?

The first thing to know is whether you are a reader or a listener. Far too few people even know that there are readers and listeners and that people are rarely both. Even fewer know which of the two they themselves are. But some examples will show how damaging such ignorance can be.

When Dwight Eisenhower was Supreme Commander of the Allied forces in Europe, he was the darling of the press. His press conferences were famous for their style—General Eisenhower showed total command of whatever question he was asked, and he was able to describe a situation and explain a policy in two or three beautifully polished and elegant sentences. Ten years later, the same journalists who had been his admirers held President Eisenhower in open contempt. He never addressed the questions, they complained, but rambled on endlessly about something else. And they constantly ridiculed him for butchering the King's English in incoherent and ungrammatical answers.

Eisenhower apparently did not know that he was a reader, not a listener. When he was Supreme Commander in Europe, his aides made sure that every question from the press was presented in writing at least half an hour before a conference was to begin. And then Eisenhower was in total command. When he became president, he succeeded two listeners, Franklin D. Roosevelt and Harry Truman. Both men knew themselves to be listeners and both enjoyed free-for-all press conferences. Eisenhower may have felt that he had to do what his two predecessors had done. As a result, he never even heard the questions journalists asked. And Eisenhower is not even an extreme case of a nonlistener.

A few years later, Lyndon Johnson destroyed his presidency, in large measure, by not knowing that he was a listener. His predecessor, John Kennedy, was a reader who had assembled a brilliant group of writers as his assistants, making sure that they wrote to him before discussing their memos in person. Johnson kept these people on his staff—and they kept on writing. He never, apparently, understood one word of what they wrote. Yet as a senator, Johnson had been superb; for parliamentarians have to be, above all, listeners.

Few listeners can be made, or can make themselves, into competent readers—and vice versa. The listener who tries to be a reader will, therefore, suffer the fate of Lyndon Johnson, whereas the reader who tries to be a listener will suffer the fate of Dwight Eisenhower. They will not perform or achieve.

How do I learn?
The second thing to know about how one performs is to know how one learns. Many first-class writers—Winston Churchill is but one example—do poorly in school. They tend to remember their schooling as pure torture. Yet few of their classmates remember it the same way. They may not have enjoyed the school very much, but the worst they suffered was boredom. The explanation is that writers do not, as a rule, learn by listening and reading. They learn by writing. Because schools do not allow them to learn this way, they get poor grades.

Schools everywhere are organized on the assumption that there is only one right way to learn and that it is the same way for everybody. But to be forced to learn the way a school teaches is sheer hell for students who learn differently. Indeed, there are probably half a dozen different ways to learn.

There are people, like Churchill, who learn by writing. Some people learn by taking copious notes. Beethoven, for example, left behind an enormous number of sketchbooks, yet he said he never actually looked at them when he composed. Asked why he kept them, he is reported to have replied, "If I don't write it down immediately, I forget it right away. If I put it into a sketchbook, I never forget it and I never have to look it up again." Some people learn by doing. Others learn by hearing themselves talk.

A chief executive I know who converted a small and mediocre family business into the leading company in its industry was one of those people who learn by talking. He was in the habit of calling his entire senior staff into his office once a week and then talking at them for two or three hours. He would raise policy issues and argue three different positions on each one. He rarely asked his associates for comments or questions; he simply needed an audience to hear himself talk. That's how he learned. And although he is a fairly extreme case, learning through talking is by no means an unusual method. Successful trial lawyers learn the same way, as do many medical diagnosticians (and so do I).

Of all the important pieces of self-knowledge, understanding how you learn is the easiest to acquire. When I ask people, "How do you learn?" most of them know the answer. But when I ask, "Do you act on this knowledge?" few answer yes. And yet, acting on this knowledge is the key to performance; or rather, *not* acting on this knowledge condemns one to nonperformance.

Am I a reader or a listener? and How do I learn? are the first questions to ask. But they are by no means the only ones. To manage yourself effectively, you also have to ask, Do I work well with people, or am I a loner? And if you do work well with people, you then must ask, In what relationship?

Some people work best as subordinates. General George Patton, the great American military hero of World War II, is a prime example. Patton was America's top troop commander. Yet when he was proposed for an independent command, General George Marshall, the U.S. chief of staff—and probably the most successful picker of men in U.S. history—said, "Patton is the best subordinate the American army has ever produced, but he would be the worst commander."

Some people work best as team members. Others work best alone. Some are exceptionally talented as coaches and mentors; others are simply incompetent as mentors.

Another crucial question is, Do I produce results as a decision maker or as an adviser? A great many people perform best as advisers but cannot take the burden and pressure of making the decision. A good many other people, by contrast, need an adviser to force themselves to think; then they can make decisions and act on them with speed, self-confidence, and courage.

This is a reason, by the way, that the number two person in an organization often fails when promoted to the number one position. The top spot requires a decision maker. Strong decision makers often put somebody they trust into the number two spot as their adviser—and in that position the person is outstanding. But in the number one spot, the same person fails. He or she knows what the decision should be but cannot accept the responsibility of actually making it.

Other important questions to ask include, Do I perform well under stress, or do I need a highly structured and predictable environment? Do I work best in a big organization or a small one? Few people work well in all kinds of environments. Again and again, I have seen people who were very successful in large organizations flounder miserably when they moved into smaller ones. And the reverse is equally true.

The conclusion bears repeating: Do not try to change yourself—you are unlikely to succeed. But work hard to improve the way you perform. And try not to take on work you cannot perform or will only perform poorly.

What Are My Values?

To be able to manage yourself, you finally have to ask, What are my values? This is not a question of ethics. With respect to ethics, the rules are the same for everybody, and the test is a simple one. I call it the "mirror test."

In the early years of this century, the most highly respected diplomat of all the great powers was the German ambassador in London. He was clearly destined for great things—to become his country's foreign minister, at least, if not its federal chancellor. Yet in 1906 he abruptly resigned rather than preside over a dinner given by the diplomatic corps for Edward VII. The king was a notorious womanizer and made it clear what kind of dinner he wanted. The ambassador is reported to have said, "I refuse to see a pimp in the mirror in the morning when I shave."

That is the mirror test. Ethics requires that you ask yourself, What kind of person do I want to see in the mirror in the morning? What is ethical behavior in one kind of organization or situation is ethical behavior in another. But ethics is only part of a value system—especially of an organization's value system.

To work in an organization whose value system is unacceptable or incompatible with one's own condemns a person both to frustration and to nonperformance.

Consider the experience of a highly successful human resources executive whose company was acquired by a bigger organization. After the acquisition, she was promoted to do the kind of work she did best, which included selecting people for important positions. The executive deeply believed that a company should hire people for such positions from the outside only after exhausting all the inside possibilities. But her new company believed in first looking outside "to bring in fresh blood." There is something to be said for both approaches—in my experience, the proper one is to do some of both. They are, however, fundamentally incompatible—not as policies but as values. They bespeak different views of the relationship between organizations and people; different views of the responsibility of an organization to its people and their development; and different views of a person's most important contribution to an enterprise. After several years of frustration, the executive quit—at considerable financial loss. Her values and the values of the organization simply were not compatible.

Similarly, whether a pharmaceutical company tries to obtain results by making constant, small improvements or by achieving occasional, highly expensive, and risky "breakthroughs" is not primarily an economic question. The results of either strategy may be pretty much the same. At bottom, there is a conflict between a value system that sees the company's contribution in terms of helping physicians do better what they already do and a value system that is oriented toward making scientific discoveries.

Whether a business should be run for short-term results or with a focus on the long term is likewise a question of values. Financial analysts believe that businesses can be run for both simultaneously. Successful businesspeople know better. To be sure, every company has to produce short-term results. But in any conflict between short-term results and long-term growth, each company will determine its own priority. This is not primarily a disagreement about economics. It is fundamentally a value conflict regarding the function of a business and the responsibility of management.

Value conflicts are not limited to business organizations. One of the fastest-growing pastoral churches in the United States measures success by the number of new parishioners. Its leadership believes that what matters is how many newcomers join the congregation. The Good Lord will then minister to their spiritual needs or at least to the needs of a sufficient percentage. Another pastoral, evangelical church believes that what matters is people's spiritual growth. The church eases out newcomers who join but do not enter into its spiritual life.

Again, this is not a matter of numbers. At first glance, it appears that the second church grows more slowly. But it retains a far larger proportion of newcomers than the first one does. Its growth, in other words, is more solid. This is also not a theological problem, or only secondarily so. It is a problem about values. In a public debate, one pastor argued, "Unless you first come to church, you will never find the gate to the Kingdom of Heaven."

"No," answered the other. "Until you first look for the gate to the Kingdom of Heaven, you don't belong in church."

Organizations, like people, have values. To be effective in an organization, a person's values must be compatible with the organization's values. They do not need to be the same, but they must be close enough to coexist. Otherwise, the person will not only be frustrated but also will not produce results.

A person's strengths and the way that person performs rarely conflict; the two are complementary. But there is sometimes a conflict between a person's values and his or her strengths. What one does well—even very well and successfully—may not fit with one's value system. In that case, the work may not appear to be worth devoting one's life to (or even a substantial portion thereof).

If I may, allow me to interject a personal note. Many years ago, I too had to decide between my values and what I was doing successfully. I was doing very well as a young investment banker in London in the mid-1930s, and the work clearly fit my strengths. Yet I did not see myself making a contribution as an asset manager. People, I realized, were what I valued, and I saw no point in being the richest man in the cemetery. I had no money and no other job prospects. Despite the continuing Depression, I quit—and it was the right thing to do. Values, in other words, are and should be the ultimate test.

Where Do I Belong?

A small number of people know very early where they belong. Mathematicians, musicians, and cooks, for instance, are usually mathematicians, musicians, and cooks by the time they are four or five years old. Physicians usually decide on their careers in their teens, if not earlier. But most people, especially highly gifted people, do not really know where they belong until they are well past their mid-twenties. By that time, however, they should know the answers to the three questions: What are my strengths? How do I perform? and, What are my values? And then they can and should decide where they belong.

Or rather, they should be able to decide where they do *not* belong. The person who has learned that he or she does not perform well in a big organization should have learned to say no to a position in one. The person who has learned that he or she is not a decision maker should have learned to say no to a decision-making assignment. A General Patton (who probably never learned this himself) should have learned to say no to an independent command.

Equally important, knowing the answer to these questions enables a person to say to an opportunity, an offer, or an assignment, "Yes, I will do that. But this is the way I should be doing it. This is the way it should be structured. This is the way the relationships should be. These are the kind of results you should expect from me, and in this time frame, because this is who I am."

Successful careers are not planned. They develop when people are prepared for opportunities because they know their strengths, their method of work, and their values. Knowing where one belongs can transform an ordinary person—hardworking and competent but otherwise mediocre—into an outstanding performer.

What Should I Contribute?

Throughout history, the great majority of people never had to ask the question, What should I contribute? They were told what to contribute, and their tasks were dictated either by the work itself—as it was for the peasant or artisan—or by a master or a mistress—as it was for domestic servants. And until very recently, it was taken for granted that most people were subordinates who did as they were told. Even in the 1950s and 1960s, the new knowledge workers (the so-called organization men) looked to their company's personnel department to plan their careers.

Then in the late 1960s, no one wanted to be told what to do any longer. Young men and women began to ask, What do *I* want to do? And what they heard was that the way to contribute was to "do your own thing." But this solution was as wrong as the organization men's had been. Very few of the people who believed that doing one's own thing would lead to contribution, self-fulfillment, and success achieved any of the three.

But still, there is no return to the old answer of doing what you are told or assigned to do. Knowledge workers in particular have to learn to ask a question that has not been asked before: What *should* my contribution be? To answer it, they must address three distinct elements: What does the situation require? Given my strengths, my way of performing, and my values, how can I make the greatest contribution to what needs to be done? And finally, What results have to be achieved to make a difference?

Consider the experience of a newly appointed hospital administrator. The hospital was big and prestigious, but it had been coasting on its reputation for 30 years. The new administrator decided that his contribution should be to establish a standard of excellence in one important area within two years. He chose to focus on the emergency room, which was big, visible, and sloppy. He decided that every patient who came into the ER had to be seen by a qualified nurse within 60 seconds. Within 12 months, the hospital's emergency room had become a model for all hospitals in the United States, and within another two years, the whole hospital had been transformed.

As this example suggests, it is rarely possible—or even particularly fruitful—to look too far ahead. A plan can usually cover no more than 18 months and still be reasonably clear and specific. So the question in most cases should be, Where and how can I achieve results that will make a difference within the next year and a half? The answer must balance several things. First, the results should be hard to achieve—they should require "stretching," to use the current buzzword. But also, they should be within reach. To aim at results that cannot be achieved—or that can be only under the most unlikely circumstances—is not being ambitious; it is being foolish. Second, the results should be meaningful. They should make a difference. Finally, results should be visible and, if at all possible, measurable. From this will come a course of action: what to do, where and how to start, and what goals and deadlines to set.

Responsibility for Relationships

Very few people work by themselves and achieve results by themselves—a few great artists, a few great scientists, a few great athletes. Most people work with others and are effective with other people. That is true whether they are members of an organization or independently employed. Managing yourself requires taking responsibility for relationships. This has two parts.

The first is to accept the fact that other people are as much individuals as you yourself are. They perversely insist on behaving like human beings. This means that they too have their strengths; they too have their ways of getting things done; they too have their values. To be effective, therefore, you have to know the strengths, the performance modes, and the values of your coworkers.

That sounds obvious, but few people pay attention to it. Typical is the person who was trained to write reports in his or her first assignment because that boss was a reader. Even if the next boss is a listener, the person goes on writing reports that, invariably, produce no results. Invariably the boss will think the employee is stupid, incompetent, and lazy, and he or she will fail. But that could have been avoided if the employee had only looked at the new boss and analyzed how *this* boss performs.

Bosses are neither a title on the organization chart nor a "function." They are individuals and are entitled to do their work in the way they do it best. It is incumbent on the people who work with them to observe them, to find out how they work, and to adapt themselves to what makes their bosses most effective. This, in fact, is the secret of "managing" the boss.

The same holds true for all your coworkers. Each works his or her way, not your way. And each is entitled to work in his or her way. What matters is whether they perform and what their values are. As for how they perform—each is likely to do it differently. The first secret of effectiveness is to understand the people you work with and depend on so that you can make use of their strengths, their ways of working, and their values. Working relationships are as much based on the people as they are on the work.

The second part of relationship responsibility is taking responsibility for communication. Whenever I, or any other consultant, start to work with an organization, the first thing I hear about are all the personality conflicts. Most of these arise from the fact that people do not know what other people are doing and how they do their work, or what contribution the other people are concentrating on and what results they expect. And the reason they do not know is that they have not asked and therefore have not been told.

This failure to ask reflects human stupidity less than it reflects human history. Until recently, it was unnecessary to tell any of these things to anybody. In the medieval city, everyone in a district plied the same trade. In the countryside, everyone in a valley planted the same crop as soon as the frost was out of the ground. Even those few people who did things that were not "common" worked alone, so they did not have to tell anyone what they were doing.

Today the great majority of people work with others who have different tasks and responsibilities. The marketing vice president may have come out of sales and know everything about sales, but she knows nothing about the things she has never done—pricing, advertising, packaging, and the like. So the people who do these things must make sure that the marketing vice president understands what they are trying to do, why they are trying to do it, how they are going to do it, and what results to expect.

If the marketing vice president does not understand what these high-grade knowledge specialists are doing, it is primarily their fault, not hers. They have not educated her. Conversely, it is the marketing vice president's responsibility to make sure that all of her coworkers understand how she looks at marketing: what her goals are, how she works, and what she expects of herself and of each one of them.

Even people who understand the importance of taking responsibility for relationships often do not communicate sufficiently with their associates. They are afraid of being thought presumptuous or inquisitive or stupid. They are wrong. Whenever someone goes to his or her associates and says, "This is what I am good at. This is how I work. These are my values. This is the contribution I plan to concentrate on and the results I should be expected to deliver," the response is always, "This is most helpful. But why didn't you tell me earlier?"

And one gets the same reaction—without exception, in my experience—if one continues by asking, "And what do I need to know about your strengths, how you perform, your values, and your proposed contribution?" In fact, knowledge workers should request this of everyone with whom they work, whether as subordinate, superior, colleague, or team member. And again, whenever this is done, the reaction is always, "Thanks for asking me. But why didn't you ask me earlier?"

Organizations are no longer built on force but on trust. The existence of trust between people does not necessarily mean that they like one another. It means that they understand one another. Taking responsibility for relationships is therefore an absolute necessity. It is a duty. Whether one is a member of the organization, a consultant to it, a supplier, or a distributor, one owes that responsibility to all one's coworkers: those whose work one depends on as well as those who depend on one's own work.

The Second Half of Your Life

When work for most people meant manual labor, there was no need to worry about the second half of your life. You simply kept on doing what you had always done. And if you were lucky enough to survive 40 years of hard work in the mill or on the railroad, you were quite happy to spend the rest of your life doing nothing. Today, however, most work is knowledge work, and knowledge workers are not "finished" after 40 years on the job, they are merely bored.

We hear a great deal of talk about the midlife crisis of the executive. It is mostly boredom. At 45, most executives have reached the peak of their business careers, and they know it. After 20 years of doing very much the same kind of work, they are very good at their jobs. But they are not learning or contributing or deriving challenge and satisfaction from the job. And yet they are still likely to face another 20 if not 25 years of work. That is why managing oneself increasingly leads one to begin a second career.

There are three ways to develop a second career. The first is actually to start one. Often this takes nothing more than moving from one kind of organization to another: The divisional controller in a large corporation, for instance, becomes the controller of a medium-sized hospital. But there are also growing numbers of people who move into different lines of work altogether: the business executive or government official who enters the ministry at 45, for instance; or the midlevel manager who leaves corporate life after 20 years to attend law school and become a small-town attorney.

We will see many more second careers undertaken by people who have achieved modest success in their first jobs. Such people have substantial skills, and they know how to work. They need a community—the house is empty with the children gone—and they need income as well. But above all, they need challenge.

The second way to prepare for the second half of your life is to develop a parallel career. Many people who are very successful in their first careers stay in the work they have been doing, either on a full-time or part-time or consulting basis. But in addition, they create a parallel job, usually in a nonprofit organization, that takes another ten hours of work a week. They might take over the administration of their church, for instance, or the presidency of the local Girl Scouts council. They might run the battered women's shelter, work as a children's librarian for the local public library, sit on the school board, and so on.

Finally, there are the social entrepreneurs. These are usually people who have been very successful in their first careers. They love their work, but it no longer challenges them. In many cases they keep on doing what they have been doing all along but spend less and less of their time on it. They also start another activity, usually a nonprofit. My friend Bob Buford, for example, built a very successful television company that he still runs. But he has also founded and built a successful nonprofit organization that works with Protestant churches, and he is building another to teach social entrepreneurs how to manage their own nonprofit ventures while still running their original businesses.

People who manage the second half of their lives may always be a minority. The majority may "retire on the job" and count the years until their actual retirement. But it is this minority, the men and women who see a long working-life expectancy as an opportunity both for themselves and for society, who will become leaders and models.

There is one prerequisite for managing the second half of your life: You must begin long before you enter it. When it first became clear 30 years ago that working-life expectancies were lengthening very fast, many observers (including myself) believed that retired people would increasingly become volunteers for nonprofit institutions. That has not happened. If one does not begin to volunteer before one is 40 or so, one will not volunteer once past 60.

Similarly, all the social entrepreneurs I know began to work in their chosen second enterprise long before they reached their peak in their original business. Consider the example of a successful lawyer, the legal counsel to a large corporation, who has started a venture to establish model schools in his state. He began to do volunteer legal work for the schools when he was around 35. He was elected to the school board at age 40. At age 50, when he had amassed a fortune, he started his own enterprise to build and to run model schools. He is, however, still working nearly full-time as the lead counsel in the company he helped found as a young lawyer.

There is another reason to develop a second major interest, and to develop it early. No one can expect to live very long without experiencing a serious setback in his or her life or work. There is the competent engineer who is passed over for promotion at age 45. There is the competent college professor who realizes at age 42 that she will never get a professorship at a big university, even though she may be fully qualified for it. There are tragedies in one's family life: the breakup of one's marriage or the loss of a child. At such times, a second major interest—not just a hobby—may make all the difference. The engineer, for example, now knows that he has not been very successful in his job. But in his outside activity—as church treasurer, for example—he is a success. One's family may break up, but in that outside activity there is still a community.

In a society in which success has become so terribly important, having options will become increasingly vital. Historically, there was no such thing as "success." The overwhelming majority of people did not expect anything but to stay in their "proper station," as an old English prayer has it. The only mobility was downward mobility.

In a knowledge society, however, we expect everyone to be a success. This is clearly an impossibility. For a great many people, there is at best an absence of failure. Wherever there is success, there has to be failure. And then it is vitally important for the individual, and equally for the individual's family, to have an area in which he or she can contribute, make a difference, and be *somebody*. That means finding a second area—whether in a second career, a parallel career, or a social venture—that offers an opportunity for being a leader, for being respected, for being a success.

The challenges of managing oneself may seem obvious, if not elementary. And the answers may seem self-evident to the point of appearing naïve. But managing oneself requires new and unprecedented things from the individual, and especially from the knowledge worker. In effect, managing oneself demands that each knowledge worker think and behave like a chief executive officer. Further, the shift from manual workers who do as they are told to knowledge workers who have to manage themselves profoundly challenges social structure. Every existing society, even the most individualistic one, takes two things for granted, if only subconsciously: that organizations outlive workers, and that most people stay put.

But today the opposite is true. Knowledge workers outlive organizations, and they are mobile. The need to manage oneself is therefore creating a revolution in human affairs.

Originally published in January 1999. Reprint R0501K

Are You a High Potential?

by Douglas A. Ready, Jay A. Conger, and Linda A. Hill

SOME EMPLOYEES ARE MORE TALENTED than others. That's a fact of organizational life that few executives and HR managers would dispute. The more debatable point is how to treat the people who appear to have the highest potential. Opponents of special treatment argue that all employees are talented in some way and, therefore, all should receive equal opportunities for growth. Devoting a disproportionate amount of energy and resources to a select few, their thinking goes, might cause you to overlook the potential contributions of the many. But the disagreement doesn't stop there. Some executives say that a company's list of high potentials—and the process for creating it—should be a closely guarded secret. After all, why dampen motivation among the roughly 95% of employees who aren't on the list?

For the past 15 to 20 years, we've been studying programs for high-potential leaders. Most recently we surveyed 45 companies worldwide about how they identify and develop these people. We then interviewed HR executives at a dozen of those companies to gain insights about the experiences they provide for high potentials and about the criteria for getting and staying on the list. Then, guided by input from HR leaders, we met with and interviewed managers they'd designated as rising stars.

Our research makes clear that high-potential talent lists exist, whether or not companies acknowledge them and whether the process for developing them is formal or informal. Of the companies we studied, 98% reported that they purposefully identify high potentials. Especially when resources are constrained, companies *do* place disproportionate attention on developing the people they think will lead their organizations into the future.

So you might be asking yourself, "How do I get—and stay—on my company's high-potential list?" This article can help you begin to answer that question. Think of it as a letter to the millions of smart, competent, hardworking, trustworthy employees who are progressing through their careers with some degree of satisfaction but are still wondering how to get where they really want to go. We'll look at the specific qualities of managers whose firms identified them as having made the grade.

The Anatomy of a High Potential

Let's begin with our definition of a high-potential employee. Your company may have a different definition or might not even officially distinguish high potentials from other employees. However, our research has shown that companies tend to think of the top 3% to 5% of their talent in these terms:

"High potentials consistently and significantly outperform their peer groups in a variety of settings and circumstances. While achieving these superior levels of performance, they exhibit behaviors that reflect their companies' culture and values in an exemplary manner. Moreover, they show a strong capacity to grow and succeed throughout their careers within an organization—more quickly and effectively than their peer groups do."

That's the basic anatomy of a high potential. Gaining membership in this elite group starts with three essential elements.

Deliver strong results—credibly.

Making your numbers is important, but it isn't enough. You'll never get on a high-potential list if you don't perform with distinction or if your results come at the expense of someone else. Competence is the baseline quality for high performance. But you also need to prove your credibility. That means building trust and confidence among your colleagues and, thereby, influencing a wide array of stakeholders.

Look at Jackie Goodwin, a bank executive cited by her HR department as a high potential. Jackie started out in the insurance division but wanted to switch to banking, which she perceived as a career path with more room for growth. Her general management skills were highly regarded, and she had a proven track record in financial services within insurance. The banking side's desire for new blood and a lack of succession planning in the region positioned her well as an outsider. Indeed, her record was as strong—if not stronger—than that of the insiders.

When Jackie was offered a stretch assignment in the banking division—a promotion to vice president and regional operating officer in Germany, the bank's second largest European operation—she accepted it, even though the odds were against her. Nobody there had heard of her, and she knew little about banking. What's more, she'd been forced on the regional president, who wanted someone with experience. Her biggest challenge was to gain credibility. The German staff was accustomed to running its own show, so Jackie figured she'd fail if she couldn't get the team on her side.

Jackie resolved to make helping her new colleagues a priority. In her first three weeks, she met with dozens of managers and openly acknowledged that she faced a steep learning curve. She also focused on achieving small wins on issues that had long been thorns in their sides. For example, she went out of her way to streamline the process for opening new accounts. As for her skeptical boss, she aimed to take as much off his plate as possible. She would ask, "What time-consuming tasks would you like to see addressed within 90 days?" Then she'd get right to work. For instance, he disliked confrontation, so Jackie tackled issues with potential for conflict, such as redesigning planning processes and resolving decision rights. She gained a reputation as a problem solver, and her influence grew steadily. Today, Jackie is the head of all commercial lending for the bank and is still considered a rising star.

Master new types of expertise.

Early in your career, getting noticed is all about mastering the technical expertise that the job requires. As you progress, you need to broaden that expertise. You start by managing an employee or a small group, and then move on to larger teams and positions (for instance, at corporate headquarters) that require you to exercise influence despite having limited formal authority. For example, in senior roles technical excellence might fade in value relative to strategic-thinking and motivational skills. At a certain point, you will face the challenge of *letting go* as much as the challenge of *adding on*. Don't aspire, for example, to be the best engineer and the best design team leader at the same time.

For some, such lessons are learned the hard way. One exceptionally talented software engineer, whom we'll call Luke, had won many accolades during a relatively short career. Confident in his potential, Luke's managers put him in charge of a team that was creating a product extension expected to attract a whole new category of users. Luke was well liked and happily took on the challenge, but he failed to recognize that technical skill alone wouldn't suffice. After several missed deadlines, company executives created a face-saving, senior-level "expert" post for him. Meanwhile, they put another technically skilled employee, who also had project-management expertise, in charge. Luke, no longer a high potential, went on to have a fairly distinguished career as a technical expert, but not in an enterprise leadership role.

Recognize that behavior counts.

Although your performance gets you noticed and promoted early in your career, your behavior is what keeps you on the radar as a high potential. Outstanding skills never really diminish in importance, but they become a given as you are expected to excel in roles with broader reach. Prospective candidates for that coveted high-potential label must demonstrate a behavioral shift from "fit and affiliation" to "role model and teacher."

The rise of general manager Phil Nolan to the executive ranks of his company, a market leader in laundry products, was due in large part to his role-model qualities. Phil was placed in charge of the

Anatomy of a High Potential

HIGH POTENTIALS ALWAYS DELIVER strong results, master new types of expertise, and recognize that behavior counts. But it's their intangible X factors that truly distinguish them from the pack.

The Four X Factors of High Potentials

1. Drive to excel
2. Catalytic learning capability
3. Enterprising spirit
4. Dynamic sensors

---

firm's troubled core product, a liquid detergent whose sales were in a multiyear downward slide. Two high-visibility marketing managers had each been given a chance to reinvigorate product sales. Both had tried price-reduction tactics, to no avail. Then it was Phil's turn. But, with a background in product development rather than marketing, he was the dark horse candidate.

Fortunately, corporate executives saw more in Phil, who had engineered a turnaround at a troubled product-development group by fostering cooperative relationships and teamwork. Highly trustworthy, he could engage people in very candid conversations about business challenges. As a result, he was able to get to the core of a problem quickly and find viable solutions. Phil not only was superb at motivating people, but also had a keen eye for patterns and an impressive strategic vision. He applied all those skills to the new assignment.

Within the first year in his new role, Phil led his team to grow product sales by 30%. In our interview with the company's HR executive, she emphasized Phil's ability to win people over: "There is humility to him despite the fact that he is now the public face of the brand. Phil helps his peers succeed rather than threatening them. He is a role model for the organization."

How High Potentials Are Hardwired

You're doing everything right. You're delivering value and early results. You're mastering new areas of expertise as you face increasingly complex challenges. You embrace your organization's culture and values. You exude confidence and have earned the respect of others. Maybe you're regularly putting in a 50-hour week and getting excellent reviews. Nevertheless, high-potential status remains elusive.

This can be infuriating because the real differentiators—what we call the "X factors"—are somewhat intangible and usually don't show up on lists of leadership competencies or on performance review forms. Here are those factors, which can tip the scales and help you achieve and maintain that coveted high-potential rating.

X FACTOR #1: A drive to excel.

High potentials aren't just high achievers. They are driven to succeed. Good, even very good, isn't good enough. Not by any stretch. They are more than willing to go that extra mile and realize they may have to make sacrifices in their personal lives in order to advance. That doesn't mean they aren't true to their values, but sheer ambition may lead them to make some pretty hard choices.

X FACTOR #2: A catalytic learning capability.

We often think of high potentials as relentless learners, but a lot of people out there learn continually yet lack an action or results orientation. The high potentials we have come across possess what we call a "catalytic learning capability." They have the capacity to scan for new ideas, the cognitive capability to absorb them, and the common sense to translate that new learning into productive action for their customers and their organizations.

X FACTOR #3: An enterprising spirit.

High potentials are always searching for productive ways to blaze new paths. They are explorers and, as such, take on the challenges of leaving their career comfort zones periodically in order to advance. It might mean a risky move—a tricky international assignment, for instance, or a cross-unit shift that demands an entirely new set of skills. Given high potentials' drive to succeed, you might think they'd be reluctant to take such a chance. But most seem to find that the advantages—the excitement and opportunity—outweigh the risks.

X FACTOR #4: Dynamic sensors.

Being driven to excel and having an enterprising spirit, combined with the urge to find new approaches, could actually become a recipe for career disaster. High potentials can get derailed for a number of reasons. They may, for instance, be tempted to impulsively accept what seems like a hot opportunity, only to find that it's a break (not a stretch) assignment or that there's no long-term career payoff. Another possibility of derailment comes from a desire to please. High potentials may avoid open disagreement with the boss or resist giving honest, potentially disappointing feedback to a peer. Successful high potentials have well-tuned radar that puts a higher premium on quality results.

Beyond judgment, high potentials possess what we call "dynamic sensors," which enable them to skirt these risks, even if just barely. They have a feel for timing, an ability to quickly read situations, and a nose for opportunity. Their enterprising spirit might otherwise lead them to make foolish decisions, but these sensors help them decide, for example, when to pursue something and when to pull back. High potentials have a knack for being in the right place at the right time.

Anatomy of an X Factor Exemplar

One of the many high potentials we met was Vineet Kapoor, described as a rising star by his bosses at Swiss medical device company Synthes. This more than $3 billion business manufactures and markets implants and biomaterials used in surgery and regeneration of the skeleton and soft tissues.

In school, long before ending up at Synthes, Vineet intended to pursue science and had a passion for improving the lives of people in emerging economies such as India. That basic vision remained with him, but his career took an unexpected path. After college, to the surprise of his peers, he chose accounting in order to gain financial expertise that would serve him well in any business career. He accepted a position with Indian professional services firm A. F. Ferguson, which had a leading portfolio of audit clients (it was eventually acquired by Deloitte in 2004). He then moved to Arthur Andersen (which merged with Ernst & Young) and eventually to KPMG in Gurgaon, India, where his then-boss was charged with leading the India practice. This move initially meant a pay cut for Vineet, but also another chance to learn about building a business.

Vineet recounted other intriguing opportunities that had opened up during his consulting career, when the Sarbanes–Oxley Act became law in the U.S. in 2002. Clients were banging down his door. Although compliance work promised handsome compensation, it didn't match his priorities of learning and effecting large-scale positive change in emerging economies. So Vineet moved to Synthes, where his X factors were evident in spades.

A drive to excel.
A drive to succeed can, well, drive some people to the brink. The key is to channel the instinct. So, for instance, Vineet decided he should always think like people one level above him. That meant asking many questions—sometimes to the consternation of his peers and bosses—but he balanced his incessant questioning with an insatiable desire to deliver. Nobody could doubt his commitment to the work and the company, and Vineet's ambition was not a matter of personal triumph. In fact, as country manager for India he created a 150-page book celebrating the contributions of his colleagues and highlighting their common values. It became something of a textbook for the Indian operation at Synthes, and employees found it illuminating. Indeed, it generated so much buzz that some employees who had left the company actually returned because the organization had been energized by it.

Vineet was not driven primarily by a wish to get ahead. His original aspiration was what fueled him. To that end he wrote an 85-page business plan that included a vision for bringing world-class education to all Indian surgeons, including those in remote areas. Synthes's CEO has said that the plan changed how the company looked at India.

Should You Tell Her She's a High Potential?

WHETHER OR NOT A COMPANY SHOULD make its list of high potentials transparent is an evergreen question. In our surveys of 45 company policies and in our work with firms during the past 15 to 20 years, we have found a growing trend toward transparency. The percentage of companies that inform high potentials of their status has risen from 70% about a decade ago to 85% today. Employers, we believe, are coming to see talent as a strategic resource that, like other types of capital, can move around. Executives are tired of exit interviews in which promising employees say, "If I had known you had plans for me and were serious about following through, I would have stayed."

Nevertheless, making your list of high potentials transparent increases the pressure to do something with the people who are on it. If you tell someone you view her as a future leader, you need to back that up with tangible progress in her professional development. Otherwise, she may feel manipulated and even lose motivation. In one case, we witnessed a near riot at a company offsite, where a group of high potentials said they felt "played"—that their status was just a retention tactic, with no real plans to promote them. Either approach has risks: If you don't make the list public, you might lose your best performers; if you opt for transparency, you'll heighten the expectation of action.

A catalytic learning capability.

When Vineet traveled to the United States for a Synthes strategy meeting, he stayed on longer to be a "fly on the wall" with the U.S. salespeople. During his stay, Vineet went with them on dozens of sales calls. Having gotten the CEO's attention with his growth strategy, Vineet thought the company would be able to execute it only with the help of more and different employees. He took what he'd learned from the U.S. sales staff to create a new salesperson competency profile for India—one that highlighted entrepreneurship, an attribute he thought would be crucial for delivering on the promise of the Indian market.

An enterprising spirit.

For Vineet, one of the toughest aspects of career growth was leaving his comfort zone, both professionally and personally. He turned down several opportunities, including one that would have required relocating to the United States. But he eventually took a post as

43

director of strategic initiatives for the Asia Pacific region, a move that forced him to leave India for Singapore. To prepare himself, Vineet agreed to a year of global rotation, spending part of his time in the U.S. corporate office and the rest in the European headquarters in Switzerland. He had to adapt his personal style and develop new strategies. He knew how to lead a team as a country manager, but supporting other country managers in achieving *their* visions was daunting. Vineet loved running his own business and having P&L responsibility; the new job meant playing a support role and getting things done through influence instead of direct control.

Dynamic sensors.

High potentials may be resented and envied as well as admired—all of which can be a source of stress. A true high potential understands this and strives to reduce animosity. Vineet certainly cared about how he was perceived. When he was first offered the country manager lead for India, at age 29, he considered turning it down because he thought others might see him as too young or inexperienced. That awareness of others' perceptions is a defining attribute of a high potential.

Developing Your X Factors

The X factors of high potentials not only don't show up in leadership competency models, but also are difficult to teach and learn, particularly in a classroom setting. Nevertheless, you can boost your odds of developing your X factors.

Becoming aware of where you're falling short is the first step. For instance, if you find yourself repeatedly getting blindsided by events, chances are your dynamic sensors aren't very strong. Some people are more attuned to their environment than others, but you can learn to improve your radar by taking simple measures such as listening to others more carefully, observing their reactions to what you say, and refreshing your network of relationships so that it better attunes you to the new businesses and markets your company is pursuing.

Three Cs for CEOs and HR Professionals

AS YOU CULTIVATE YOUR PIPELINE of high potentials, follow these principles:

Be clear with your people about the skills and behaviors that your organization needs for the future—and about why these characteristics will matter.

Be consistent in how you develop talent. Avoid adopting a "development for all" mentality when times are good but then making deep cuts when times are tight.

Be creative about the next generation. That marketing manager from Shanghai who doesn't quite fit your mold might be just the talent you need to win in the future.

Catalytic learning requires an interest in acting, not just learning. Learning without actually changing your behavior is an opportunity wasted. It may be difficult to develop more drive or an enterprising spirit, but with reflection you can begin to be more proactive or take a few more risks. This all speaks to the importance of investing time and energy in self-reflection. You must also recognize the value of seeking advice from a coach or mentor—and of figuring out where an adviser's help ends and your independence begins.

High-Potential Status Has Its Downsides

It's great to be recognized for what you can do and how you might contribute to your company's future, but high-potential status comes at a price. For starters, there's no tenure. People can—and do—fall off the list, and some remove themselves voluntarily or by default because they don't have the time or the passion for the journey. Virtually all companies we surveyed indicated that remaining a high potential is not guaranteed, and we found that anywhere from 5% to 20% drop off the rolls each year, whether by choice or not.

Among the reasons for losing a spot on the high-potential list are making a poor transition into a new role, diminished performance two years in a row, behavior that's out of line with the company's culture and values, and a significant visible failure. A dramatic fall from grace that stands out in our research involved an executive, whom we'll call Marta, who was in line for the position of chief technology officer at a leading financial services firm.

Marta was an extremely bright high-potential manager with superb technical skills. But she let her smarts get in the way. She didn't want to "waste her time" talking with other senior stakeholders whose clients needed new technology applications. She "knew the right answer" regardless of whether it met clients' needs and expectations. Her dynamic sensors and catalytic learning capability were nowhere to be found. She was intelligent but not wise, and every effort at coaching her failed. Marta was too valuable to be fired, but she was removed from the succession track, which in the end cost her a possible multimillion-dollar payout. She directed the project from a technical standpoint, but her career essentially stalled.

Being singled out for extra developmental attention also can entail sacrifices in your personal life. Some people love to change jobs often, but for others that creates an enormous amount of stress, not to mention tough family-related and other choices. People's expectations of you are high, and colleagues who aren't on the list may secretly, perhaps unconsciously, want you to falter, or even resent you enough to hope you fall from grace.

Getting on a high-potential list can be a significant growth opportunity, so it's not our intention to discourage great managers from aiming for it. However, you need to figure out not just *how* to get on the list, but *why* you want to in the first place. And that means soul-searching. Are you ready for high-potential status? Is it what you really want? If so, the rewards of obtaining it can be huge; if not, then focus on your passions in other ways. Whatever your answer, don't forget: Performance always counts; your behavior matters more and more as you grow; and those X factors are your secret weapons.

Originally published October 2006. Reprint R1006E

Making Yourself Indispensable

by John H. Zenger, Joseph R. Folkman, and Scott K. Edinger

A MANAGER WE'LL call Tom was a midlevel sales executive at a *Fortune* 500 company. After a dozen or so years there, he was thriving—he made his numbers, he was well liked, he got consistently positive reviews. He applied for a promotion that would put him in charge of a high-profile worldwide product-alignment initiative, confident that he was the top candidate and that this was the logical next move for him, a seemingly perfect fit for his skills and ambitions. His track record was solid. He'd made no stupid mistakes or career-limiting moves, and he'd had no run-ins with upper management. He was stunned, then, when a colleague with less experience got the job. What was the matter?

As far as Tom could tell, nothing. Everyone was happy with his work, his manager assured him, and a recent 360-degree assessment confirmed her view. Tom was at or above the norm in every area, strong not only in delivering results but also in problem solving, strategic thinking, and inspiring others to top performance. "No need to reinvent yourself," she said. "Just keep doing what you're doing. Go with your strengths."

But how? Tom was at a loss. Should he think more strategically? Become even more inspiring? Practice problem-solving more intently?

It's pretty easy and straightforward to improve on a weakness; you can get steady, measurable results through linear development—that is, by learning and practicing basic techniques. But the data from our decades of work with tens of thousands of executives all over the world has shown us that developing strengths is very different. Doing more of what you already do well yields only incremental improvement. To get appreciably better at it, you have to work on complementary skills—what we call *nonlinear* development. This has long been familiar to athletes as cross-training. A novice runner, for example, benefits from doing stretching exercises and running a few times a week, gradually increasing mileage to build up endurance and muscle memory. But an experienced marathoner won't get significantly faster merely by running ever longer distances. To reach the next level, he needs to supplement that regimen by building up complementary skills through weight training, swimming, bicycling, interval training, yoga, and the like.

So it is with leadership competencies. To move from good to much better, you need to engage in the business equivalent of cross-training. If you're technically adept, for instance, delving even more deeply into technical manuals won't get you nearly as far as honing a complementary skill such as communication, which will make your expertise more apparent and accessible to your coworkers.

In this article we provide a simple guide to becoming a far more effective leader. We will see how Tom identified his strengths, decided which one to focus on and which complementary skill to develop, and what the results were. The process is straightforward, but complements are not always obvious. So first we'll take a closer look at the leadership equivalent of cross-training.

The Interaction Effect

In cross-training, the combination of two activities produces an improvement—an *interaction effect*—substantially greater than either one can produce on its own. There's nothing mysterious here. Combining diet with exercise, for example, has long been known to be substantially more effective in losing weight than either diet or exercise alone.

Idea in Brief

Good leaders can become exceptional by developing just a few of their strengths to the highest level—but not by merely doing more of the same.

Instead, they need to engage in the business equivalent of cross-training—that is, to enhance complementary skills that will enable them to make fuller use of their strengths.

For example, technical skills can become more effective when communication skills improve, making a leader's expertise more apparent and more accessible.

Once a few of their strengths have reached the level of outstanding, leaders become indispensable to their organizations despite the weaknesses they may have.

In our previous research we found 16 differentiating leadership competencies that correlate strongly with positive business outcomes such as increased profitability, employee engagement, revenue, and customer satisfaction. Among those 16, we wondered, could we find pairs that would produce significant interaction effects?

We searched through our database of more than a quarter million 360-degree surveys of some 30,000 developing leaders for pairings that resulted in far higher scores on overall leadership effectiveness than either attribute did on its own. The results were unambiguous. Take, for example, the competencies "focuses on results" and "builds relationships." Only 14% of leaders who were reasonably strong (that is, scored in the 75th percentile) in focusing on results but less so in building relationships reached the extraordinary leadership level: the 90th percentile in overall leadership effectiveness. Similarly, only 12% of those who were reasonably strong in building relationships but less so in focusing on results reached that level. But when an individual performed well in both categories, something dramatic happened: Fully 72% of those in the 75th percentile in both categories reached the 90th percentile in overall leadership effectiveness.

We measured the degree of correlation between overall leadership effectiveness and all possible pairings of our 16 differentiating competencies to learn which pairings were the most powerful. We also matched our 16 competencies with other leadership skills and measured how those pairs correlated with overall leadership effectiveness. We discovered that each of the 16 has up to a dozen associated behaviors—which we call *competency companions*—that were highly correlated with leadership excellence when combined with the differentiating competency. (For a complete list of the competencies and their companions, see the exhibit "What skills will magnify my strengths?")

Consider the main competency "displays honesty and integrity." How would a leader go about improving a relative strength in this area? By being more honest? (We've heard that answer to the question many times.) That's not particularly useful advice. If an executive were weak in this area, we could recommend various ways to improve: Behave more consistently, avoid saying one thing and doing another, follow through on stated commitments, and so on. But a leader with high integrity is most likely already doing those things.

Our competency-companion research suggests a practical path forward. For example, assertiveness is among the behaviors that when paired with honesty and integrity correlate most strongly with high levels of overall leadership effectiveness. We don't mean to imply a causal relationship here: Assertiveness doesn't make someone honest, and integrity doesn't produce assertiveness. But if a highly principled leader learned to become more assertive, he might be more likely to speak up and act with the courage of his convictions, thus applying his strength more widely or frequently to become a more effective leader.

Our data suggest other ways in which a competency companion can reinforce a leadership strength. It might make the strength more apparent, as in the case of the technically strong leader who improves her ability to communicate. Or skills learned in developing the competency companion might be profitably applied to the main competency. A leader strong in innovativeness, for instance, might learn how to champion change, thus encouraging his team to achieve results in new and more creative ways.

What skills will magnify my strengths?

Our research shows that 16 leadership competencies correlate strongly with positive business outcomes. Each of them has up to a dozen "competency companions" whose development will strengthen the core skill.

Character

Displays honesty and integrity

- Shows concern and consideration for others
- Is trustworthy
- Demonstrates optimism
- Is assertive
- Inspires and motivates others
- Deals well with ambiguity
- Is decisive
- Focuses on results

Personal capability

Exhibits technical/professional expertise

- Solves problems and analyzes issues
- Builds relationships and networks
- Communicates powerfully and broadly
- Pursues excellence
- Takes initiative
- Develops others
- Displays honesty and integrity
- Acts in the team's best interest

Solves problems and analyzes issues

- Takes initiative
- Is organized and good at planning
- Is decisive
- Innovates
- Wants to tackle challenges
- Develops strategic perspective
- Acts independently
- Has technical expertise
- Communicates powerfully and broadly

Innovates

- Is willing to take risks and challenge the status quo
- Supports others in risk-taking
- Solves problems and analyzes issues
- Champions change
- Learns quickly from success and failure
- Develops strategic perspective
- Takes initiative

Practices self-development

- Listens
- Is open to others' ideas
- Respects others
- Displays honesty and integrity
- Inspires and motivates others
- Provides effective feedback and development
- Takes initiative
- Is willing to take risks and challenge the status quo

Getting results

Focuses on results

- Is organized and good at planning
- Displays honesty and integrity
- Anticipates problems
- Sees desired results clearly
- Provides effective feedback and development
- Establishes stretch goals
- Is personally accountable
- Is quick to act
- Provides rewards and recognition
- Creates a high-performance team
- Marshals adequate resources
- Innovates

Establishes stretch goals

- Inspires and motivates others
- Is willing to take risks and challenge the status quo
- Gains the support of others
- Develops strategic perspective
- Champions change
- Is decisive
- Has technical and business expertise
- Focuses on results

Takes initiative

- Anticipates problems
- Emphasizes speed
- Is organized and good at planning
- Champions others
- Deals well with ambiguity
- Follows through
- Inspires and motivates others
- Establishes stretch goals
- Displays honesty and integrity

(continued)

What skills will magnify my strengths? *(continued)*

Interpersonal skills

Communicates powerfully and broadly

- Inspires and motivates others
- Develops strategic perspective
- Establishes stretch goals
- Deals effectively with the outside world
- Is trustworthy
- Involves others
- Translates messages for clarity
- Solves problems and analyzes issues
- Takes initiative
- Innovates
- Develops others

Inspires and motivates others

- Connects emotionally with others
- Establishes stretch goals
- Exhibits clear vision and direction
- Communicates powerfully and broadly
- Develops others
- Collaborates and fosters teamwork
- Nurtures innovation
- Takes initiative
- Champions change
- Is a strong role model

Builds relationships

- Collaborates and fosters teamwork
- Displays honesty and integrity
- Develops others
- Listens
- Communicates powerfully and broadly
- Provides rewards and recognition
- Practices inclusion and values diversity
- Demonstrates optimism
- Practices self-development

Develops others

- Practices self-development
- Shows concern and consideration for others
- Is motivated by the success of others
- Practices inclusion and values diversity
- Develops strategic perspective
- Provides effective feedback and development
- Inspires and motivates others

- Innovates
- Provides rewards and recognition
- Displays honesty and integrity

Collaborates and fosters teamwork

- Is trustworthy
- Builds relationships and networks
- Practices inclusion and values diversity
- Develops strategic perspective
- Establishes stretch goals
- Communicates powerfully and broadly
- Displays honesty and integrity
- Adapts to change
- Inspires and motivates others
- Develops others

Leading change

Develops strategic perspective

- Focuses on customers
- Innovates
- Solves problems and analyzes issues
- Communicates powerfully and broadly
- Establishes stretch goals
- Demonstrates business acumen
- Champions change
- Inspires and motivates others

Champions change

- Inspires and motivates others
- Builds relationships and networks
- Develops others
- Provides rewards and recognition
- Practices inclusion and values diversity
- Innovates
- Focuses on results
- Is willing to take risks and challenge the status quo
- Develops strategic perspective

Connects the group to the outside world

- Develops broad perspective
- Develops strategic perspective
- Inspires and motivates others
- Has strong interpersonal skills
- Takes initiative
- Gathers and assimilates information
- Champions change
- Communicates powerfully and broadly

Building Strengths, Step by Step

As a practical matter, cross-training for leadership skills is clear-cut: (1) Identify your strengths. (2) Choose a strength to focus on according to its importance to the organization and how passionately you feel about it. (3) Select a complementary behavior you'd like to enhance. (4) Develop it in a linear way.

Identify your strengths

Strengths can arguably be identified in a variety of ways. But we contend that in the context of effective leadership, your view of your own (or even some perfectly objective view, supposing one could be had) is less important than other people's, because leadership is all about your effect on others. That's why we start with a 360—as Tom did.

Ideally, you should go about this in a psychometrically valid way, through a formal process in which you and your direct reports, peers, and bosses anonymously complete questionnaires ranking your leadership attributes on a quantitative scale. You and they should also answer some qualitative, open-ended questions concerning your strengths, your fatal flaws (if any), and the relative importance of those attributes to the company. By "fatal flaws," we mean flaws so critical that they can overpower any strengths you have or may develop—flaws that can derail your career.

Not every organization is able or willing to conduct 360s for everyone. So if that's not feasible, you may be able to solicit qualitative data from your colleagues if—and this is a big caveat—you can make them feel comfortable enough to be honest in their feedback. You could create your own feedback form and ask people to return it anonymously. (See the sidebar "An Informal 360" for a suggested set of questions.) We have also seen earnest one-on-one conversations work for this purpose; if nothing else, they show your coworkers that you are genuinely interested in self-improvement. (Nevertheless, it's unlikely that anyone will tell you directly if you have fatal flaws.)

In interpreting the results, people commonly focus first on their lowest scores. But unless those are extremely low (in the 10th percentile),

An Informal 360

BEFORE YOU CAN BUILD ON YOUR STRENGTHS, you need an objective view of what they are. Ideally, this comes from a formal, confidential 360-degree evaluation. But if that's not possible, a direct approach can work. Try simply asking your team members, colleagues, and boss these simple questions, either in person or in writing.

- What leadership skills do you think are strengths for me?

- Is there anything I do that might be considered a fatal flaw—that could derail my career or lead me to fail in my current job if it's not addressed?

- What leadership ability, if outstanding, would have the most significant impact on the productivity or effectiveness of the organization?

- What leadership abilities of mine have the most significant impact on you?

Do your best to exhibit receptiveness and to create a feeling of safety (especially for direct reports). Make it clear that you're seeking self-improvement. Tell your colleagues explicitly that you are open to negative feedback and that you will absorb it professionally and appropriately—and without retribution. Of course, you need to follow through on this promise, or the entire process will fail.

---

that's a mistake. (We have found that 20% of executives do typically discover such a critical problem in their 360s; if you're among them, you must fix the flaw, which you can do in a linear way.)

What makes leaders indispensable to their organizations, our data unmistakably show, is not being good at many things but being uniquely outstanding at a few things. Such strengths allow a leader's inevitable weaknesses to be overlooked. The executives in our database who exhibited no profound (that is, in the 90th percentile) strengths scored only in the 34th percentile, on average, in overall leadership effectiveness. But if they had just one outstanding strength, their overall leadership effectiveness score rose to the 64th percentile, on average. In other words, the difference between being in the bottom third of leaders and being almost in the top third is a single extraordinary strength. Two profound strengths put leaders close to the top quartile, three put them in the top quintile, and four

What difference can a single strength make?

Raising just one competency to the level of outstanding can up your overall leadership effectiveness ranking from the bottom third to almost the top third.

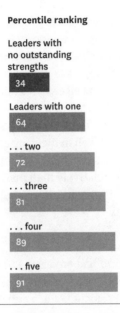

Percentile ranking

Leaders with
no outstanding
strengths
34

Leaders with one
64

. . . two
72

. . . three
81

. . . four
89

. . . five
91

put them nearly in the top decile. (See the exhibit "What difference can a single strength make?")

In this context, a look at Tom's 360 results sheds light on the question of why he was passed over for a plum assignment. Tom had no critical flaws, but he hadn't yet demonstrated any outstanding strengths either. With no strengths above the 70th percentile, he didn't score "good," let alone "outstanding," in overall leadership ability. Anyone in the organization with a single notable strength was likely to outpace him for promotion opportunities. But if Tom could lift just a few of his relative strengths from the 70th to the 80th and then the 90th percentile, his overall leadership effectiveness might go from above average to good to exceptional. Clearly, those strengths merited a closer examination.

Like many people, though, Tom was initially galvanized by the low bars on his chart, which evoked a mixture of guilt and denial. His relatively low score on building relationships called up uncomfortable memories of high school—something he didn't mention as he looked over the results with his boss. But he did say that he couldn't believe he wasn't scored higher on innovativeness, and he started to tick off initiatives he felt he deserved credit for. Maybe he was innovative, and maybe he wasn't. It's common for your self-assessment to vary sharply from everyone else's assessment of you. But remember that it's others' opinions that matter.

When Tom did turn his attention to his strengths, he wasn't surprised to see that he scored well in focusing on results and in solving problems and analyzing issues. Less obvious to him, and perhaps more gratifying, were his relatively high marks in developing strategic perspective and inspiring and motivating others. Now he could move on to the next step.

Choose a strength to focus on

Choices between good and bad are easy. But choices between good and good cause us to deliberate and second-guess. It may not matter which competency Tom selected, since enhancing any one of them would markedly improve his leadership effectiveness. Nevertheless, we recommend that developing leaders focus on a competency that matters to the organization and about which they feel some passion, because a strength you feel passionate about that is not important to your organization is essentially a hobby, and a strength the organization needs that you don't feel passionate about is just a chore.

You can use your colleagues' importance ratings from the 360 assessment to get a somewhat objective view of organizational needs. But the prospect of following his passions alarmed Tom, who didn't know how to begin. Answering a series of questions made the notion more concrete. For each of the 16 competencies, he ran down the following list:

- Do I look for ways to enhance this skill?

- Do I look for new ways to use it?

- Am I energized, not exhausted, when I use it?

- Do I pursue projects in which I can apply this strength?

- Can I imagine devoting time to improving it?

- Would I enjoy getting better at this skill?

Counting his "yes" answers gave Tom a solid way to quantify his passions. A simple worksheet showed him how his skills, his passions, and the organization's needs dovetailed (see the exhibit "Narrowing down the options"). When Tom checked off his top five competencies, his five passions, and the organization's top priorities, he could see a clear convergence. He decided to focus on the strength that, as it happens, we have found to be most universally associated with extraordinary leadership: "inspires and motivates others."

Select a complementary behavior

People who excel at motivating others are good at persuading them to take action and to go the extra mile. They effectively exercise power to influence key decisions for the benefit of the organization. They know how to motivate different people in different ways. So it was not surprising that Tom already did those things pretty well. He scanned the list of competency companions:

- Connects emotionally with others

- Establishes stretch goals

- Exhibits clear vision and direction

- Communicates powerfully and broadly

- Develops others

- Collaborates and fosters teamwork

- Nurtures innovation

- Takes initiative

- Champions change

- Is a strong role model

Narrowing down the options

The strength you focus on should be both important to the organization and important to you. A simple worksheet (like Tom's, below) can help you see where your strengths and interests and the needs of your organization converge. Choose five competencies in each of the three categories.

	Your competencies	Your passions	Organizational needs	Total
1. Displays honesty and integrity				
2. Exhibits technical/professional expertise	X			1
3. Solves problems and analyzes issues	X			1
4. Innovates		X	X	2
5. Practices self-development				
6. Focuses on results	X			1
7. Establishes stretch goals				
8. Takes initiative		X		1
9. Communicates powerfully and broadly			X	1
10. Inspires and motivates others	X	X	X	③
11. Builds relationships			X	1
12. Develops others		X		1
13. Collaborates and fosters teamwork		X		1
14. Develops strategic perspective	X		X	2
15. Champions change				
16. Connects the group to the outside world				

You should choose a companion behavior that, like a good strength, is important to the organization and makes you feel enthusiastic about tackling it. But at this point it's also constructive to consider your lower scores. In talking these points over with his manager, Tom decided to work on his communication skills, which didn't score particularly high but were high enough that raising them a little could make a significant difference.

Develop it in a linear way

Having settled on a competency companion, Tom could now work at directly improving his basic skills in that area. Strong communicators speak concisely and deliver effective presentations. Their instructions are clear. They write well. They can explain new concepts clearly. They help people understand how their work contributes to broader business objectives. They can translate terms used by people in different functions. Tom saw lots of room for improvement here: No one would ever call him concise; he didn't always finish sentences he'd started; and he found writing a challenge.

We would have recommended that he look for as many opportunities as possible, both inside and outside work, to improve his communication. He could take a course in business writing. He could practice with friends and family, in his church or his community. He could volunteer to make presentations to senior management or ask colleagues to critique some of his memos and e-mails. He might volunteer to help high school students write college application essays. He could videotape himself making speeches or join a local Toastmasters club.

Tom decided to seek the advice of a colleague whose communication skills he admired. The colleague suggested (among other things) that because writing was not a strong point, Tom should practice communicating more in person or over the phone. This turned out to be challenging: Tom found that before he could even begin, he had to change his approach to e-mail, because he was in the habit of constantly checking and replying to it throughout the day. He couldn't always substitute the phone, because he couldn't make calls while he was in a meeting or talking to someone else. He started to set aside specific times of the day for e-mail so that he could reply by phone or in person—a small change that had unexpected consequences. Instead of being interrupted and distracted at random moments throughout the day (and evening), his staffers had concentrated, direct interactions with him. They found these more efficient and effective, even though they could no longer choose when (or whether) to reply to Tom's cryptic e-mails. Tom found that he connected better with people he talked to, both because his attention wasn't divided between them and his BlackBerry and because he could read their tone of voice and body language. As a result, he absorbed more information, and his colleagues felt he was more attentive to their views.

Tom also started to pay more attention not just to how he was communicating but to what he was saying. His colleague suggested that Tom start to keep track of how often he issued instructions versus how often he asked questions. Tom also took note of how much of what he said was criticism (constructive or otherwise) and how much was encouragement. Increasing the proportion of questions and encouragement had an immediate effect: His team began to understand him more quickly, so he didn't have to repeat himself as often. Several team members actually thanked him for allowing them to express their points of view.

Like Tom, you should expect to see some concrete evidence of improvement within 30 to 60 days. If you don't, what you're doing is not working. That said, complementary behaviors improve steadily with practice, and Tom's progress is typical: Fifteen months later, on taking another 360, he found he'd moved into the 82nd percentile in his ability to inspire. He wasn't extraordinary yet, but he was getting close. Our advice would be to keep at it—to improve another competency companion or two until he reaches the 90th percentile and becomes truly exceptional at inspiring others. Then he can start the entire process again with another strength and its complements, and another—at which point he will be making a uniquely valuable contribution to his company.

Can You Overdo It?

Everyone knows someone who is too assertive, too technically oriented, too focused on driving for results. Many people cite examples like these to argue against the wisdom of improving your leadership effectiveness by strengthening your strengths. Our research does in fact show a point where balance becomes important. The data suggest that the difference between having four profound strengths and having five is a gain of merely 2 percentage points in overall leadership effectiveness. Thus leaders who are already exceptional should consider one more variable.

You will note in the exhibit "What skills will magnify my strengths?" that the 16 differentiating competencies fall into five broader categories: character, personal capability, getting results, interpersonal skills, and leading change. People who have many strengths should consider how they are distributed across those categories and focus improvement efforts on an underrepresented one.

But we cannot think of a less constructive approach to improving your leadership effectiveness than treating your strengths as weaknesses. Have you ever known anyone who had too much integrity? Was too effective a communicator? Was just too inspiring? Developing competency companions works precisely because, rather than simply doing more of the same, you are enhancing how you already behave with new ways of working and interacting that will make that behavior more effective.

———

Focusing on your strengths is hardly a new idea. Forty-four years ago Peter Drucker made the business case eloquently in *The Effective Executive:* "Unless . . . an executive looks for strength and works at making strength productive, he will only get the impact of what a man cannot do, of his lacks, his weaknesses, his impediments to performance and effectiveness. To staff from what there is not and to focus on weakness is wasteful—a misuse, if not abuse, of the human resource." Since then a body of work has grown up supporting and advocating for Drucker's approach. Our own research shows how big a difference developing a few strengths can make. It is distressing to find that fewer than 10% of the executives we work with have any plan to do so.

We are convinced that the problem is less a matter of conviction than of execution. Executives need a path to enhancing their strengths that is as clear as the one to fixing their weaknesses. That is the greatest value, we believe, of the cross-training approach: It allows people to use the linear improvement techniques they know and understand to produce a nonlinear result.

Often executives complain to us that there are not enough good leaders in their organizations. We would argue that in fact far too many leaders are merely good. The challenge is not to replace bad leaders with good ones; it is to turn people like Tom—hardworking, capable executives who are reasonably good at their jobs—into outstanding leaders with distinctive strengths.

Originally published in October 2011. Reprint R1110E

How to Play to Your Strengths

by Laura Morgan Roberts, Gretchen Spreitzer, Jane Dutton, Robert Quinn, Emily Heaphy, and Brianna Barker Caza

MOST FEEDBACK ACCENTUATES THE NEGATIVE. During formal employee evaluations, discussions invariably focus on "opportunities for improvement," even if the overall evaluation is laudatory. Informally, the sting of criticism lasts longer than the balm of praise. Multiple studies have shown that people pay keen attention to negative information. For example, when asked to recall important emotional events, people remember four negative memories for every positive one. No wonder most executives give and receive performance reviews with all the enthusiasm of a child on the way to the dentist.

Traditional, corrective feedback has its place, of course; every organization must filter out failing employees and ensure that everyone performs at an expected level of competence. Unfortunately, feedback that ferrets out flaws can lead otherwise talented managers to overinvest in shoring up or papering over their perceived weaknesses, or forcing themselves onto an ill-fitting template. Ironically, such a focus on problem areas prevents companies from reaping the best performance from its people. After all, it's a rare baseball player who is equally good at every position. Why should a natural third baseman labor to develop his skills as a right fielder?

The alternative, as the Gallup Organization researchers Marcus Buckingham, Donald Clifton, and others have suggested, is to foster excellence in the third baseman by identifying and harnessing his unique strengths. It is a paradox of human psychology that while people remember criticism, they respond to praise. The former makes them defensive and therefore unlikely to change, while the latter produces confidence and the desire to perform better. Managers who build up their strengths can reach their highest potential. This positive approach does not pretend to ignore or deny the problems that traditional feedback mechanisms identify. Rather, it offers a separate and unique feedback experience that counterbalances negative input. It allows managers to tap into strengths they may or may not be aware of and so contribute more to their organizations.

During the past few years, we have developed a powerful tool to help people understand and leverage their individual talents. Called the Reflected Best Self (RBS) exercise, our method allows managers to develop a sense of their "personal best" in order to increase their future potential. The RBS exercise is but one example of new approaches springing from an area of research called positive organizational scholarship (POS). Just as psychologists know that people respond better to praise than to criticism, organizational behavior scholars are finding that when companies focus on positive attributes such as resilience and trust, they can reap impressive bottom-line returns. (For more on this research, visit the Center for Positive Organizations.) Thousands of executives, as well as tomorrow's leaders enrolled in business schools around the world, have completed the RBS exercise.

In this article, we will walk you through the RBS exercise step-by-step and describe the insights and results it can yield. Before we proceed, however, a few caveats are in order. First, understand that the tool is not designed to stroke your ego; its purpose is to assist you in developing a plan for more effective action. (Without such a plan, you'll keep running in place.) Second, the lessons generated from the RBS exercise can elude you if you don't pay sincere attention to them. If you are too burdened by time pressures and job demands, you may just file the information away and forget about

Idea in Brief

Most feedback accentuates the negative. During formal employee evaluations, discussions invariably focus on "opportunities for improvement," even if the overall evaluation is laudatory. No wonder most executives—and their direct reports—dread them.

Traditional, corrective feedback has its place, of course; every organization must filter out failing employees and ensure that everyone performs at an expected level of competence. But too much emphasis on problem areas prevents companies from reaping the best from their people. After all, it's a rare baseball player who is equally good at every position. Why should a natural third baseman labor to develop his skills as a right fielder?

This article presents a tool to help you understand and leverage your strengths. Called the Reflected Best Self (RBS) exercise, it offers a unique feedback experience that counterbalances negative input. It

allows you to tap into talents you may or may not be aware of and so increase your career potential.

To begin the RBS exercise, you first need to solicit comments from family, friends, colleagues, and teachers, asking them to give specific examples of times in which those strengths were particularly beneficial. Next, you need to search for common themes in the feedback, organizing them in a table to develop a clear picture of your strong suits. Third, you must write a self-portrait—a description of yourself that summarizes and distills the accumulated information. And finally, you need to redesign your personal job description to build on what you're good at.

The RBS exercise will help you discover who you are at the top of your game. Once you're aware of your best self, you can shape the positions you choose to play—both now and in the next phase of your career.

it. To be effective, the exercise requires commitment, diligence, and follow-through. It may even be helpful to have a coach keep you on task. Third, it's important to conduct the RBS exercise at a different time of year than the traditional performance review so that negative feedback from traditional mechanisms doesn't interfere with the results of the exercise.

Used correctly, the RBS exercise can help you tap into unrecognized and unexplored areas of potential. Armed with a constructive, systematic process for gathering and analyzing data about your best self, you can burnish your performance at work.

Step 1: Identify Respondents and Ask for Feedback

The first task in the exercise is to collect feedback from a variety of people inside and outside work. By gathering input from a variety of sources—family members, past and present colleagues, friends, teachers, and so on—you can develop a much broader and richer understanding of yourself than you can from a standard performance evaluation.

As we describe the process of the Reflected Best Self exercise, we will highlight the experience of Robert Duggan (not his real name), whose self-discovery process is typical of the managers we've observed. Having retired from a successful career in the military at a fairly young age and earned an MBA from a top business school, Robert accepted a midlevel management position at an IT services firm. Despite strong credentials and leadership experience, Robert remained stuck in the same position year after year. His performance evaluations were generally good but not strong enough to put him on the high-potential track. Disengaged, frustrated, and disheartened, Robert grew increasingly stressed and disillusioned with his company. His workday felt more and more like an episode of *Survivor.*

Seeking to improve his performance, Robert enrolled in an executive education program and took the RBS exercise. As part of the exercise, Robert gathered feedback from 11 individuals from his past and present who knew him well. He selected a diverse but balanced group—his wife and two other family members, two friends from his MBA program, two colleagues from his time in the army, and four current colleagues.

Robert then asked these individuals to provide information about his strengths, accompanied by specific examples of moments when Robert used those strengths in ways that were meaningful to them, to their families or teams, or to their organizations. Many people—Robert among them—feel uncomfortable asking for exclusively positive feedback, particularly from colleagues. Accustomed to hearing about their strengths and weaknesses simultaneously,

Requesting Feedback

HERE'S SOME SAMPLE LANGUAGE to use as you solicit feedback from family, friends, teachers, and colleagues.

Dear Colleague,

I'm currently working on creating a personal development plan. As part of that process, I'm gathering feedback from a variety of people I work with closely to help me develop a broader understanding of the strengths I bring to our work. I'm hoping you'll be willing to share your thoughts with me.

From your perspective, what would you say my professional strengths are? Just two or three would be helpful, and if you could cite specific examples of situations where I used those in ways that were meaningful to you, that would be great. Your candid feedback and examples will help me shape my development plan.

Thank you for taking the time to help me.

Sincerely,
X

many executives imagine any positive feedback will be unrealistic, even false. Some also worry that respondents might construe the request as presumptuous or egotistical. But once managers accept that the exercise will help them improve their performance, they tend to dive in.

Within ten days, Robert received e-mail responses from all 11 people describing specific instances when he had made important contributions—including pushing for high quality under a tight deadline, being inclusive in communicating with a diverse group, and digging for critical information. The answers he received surprised him. As a military veteran and a technical person holding an MBA, Robert rarely yielded to his emotions. But in reading story after story from his respondents, Robert found himself deeply moved—as if he were listening to appreciative speeches at a party thrown in his honor. The stories were also surprisingly convincing. He had more strengths than he knew. (For more on Step 1, refer to the sidebar "Gathering Feedback.")

Gathering Feedback

A CRITICAL STEP in the Reflected Best Self exercise involves soliciting feedback from family, friends, teachers, and colleagues. E-mail is an effective way of doing this, not only because it's comfortable and fast but also because it's easy to cut and paste responses into an analysis table such as the one in the main body of this article.

Below is the feedback Robert, a manager we observed, received from a current colleague and from a former coworker in the army.

From: Amy Chen

To: Robert Duggan

Subject: Re: Request for feedback

Dear Robert,

One of the greatest ways that you add value is that you stand for doing the right thing. For example, I think of the time that we were behind on a project for a major client and quality began to slip. You called a meeting and suggested that we had a choice: We could either pull a C by satisfying the basic requirements, or we could pull an A by doing excellent work. You reminded us that we could contribute to a better outcome. In the end, we met our deadline, and the client was very happy with the result.

From: Mike Bruno

To: Robert Duggan

Subject: Re: Request for feedback

One of the greatest ways you add value is that you persist in the face of adversity. I remember the time that we were both leading troops under tight security. We were getting conflicting information from the ground and from headquarters. You pushed to get the ground and HQ folks to talk to each other despite the tight time pressure. That information saved all of our lives. You never lost your calm, and you never stopped expecting or demanding the best from everyone involved.

Step 2: Recognize Patterns

In this step, Robert searched for common themes among the feedback, adding to the examples with observations of his own, then organizing all the input into a table. (To view parts of Robert's table, see the exhibit "Finding common themes.") Like many who participate in the RBS exercise, Robert expected that, given the diversity of respondents, the comments he received would be inconsistent or even competing. Instead, he was struck by their uniformity. The comments from his wife and family members were similar to those

Finding common themes

Creating a table helps you make sense of the feedback you collect. By clustering examples, you can more easily compare responses and identify common themes.

Common theme	Examples given	Possible interpretation
Ethics, values, and courage	• I take a stand when superiors and peers cross the boundaries of ethical behavior. • I am not afraid to stand up for what I believe in. I confront people who litter or who yell at their kids in public.	• I am at my best when I choose the harder right over the easier wrong. I derive even more satisfaction when I am able to teach others. I am professionally courageous.
Curiosity and perseverance	• I gave up a promising career in the military to get my MBA. • I investigated and solved a security breach through an innovative approach.	• I like meeting new challenges. I take risks and persevere despite obstacles.
Ability to build teams	• In high school, I assembled a team of students that helped improve the school's academic standards. • I am flexible and willing to learn from others, and I give credit where credit is due.	• I thrive when working closely with others.

from his army buddies and work colleagues. Everyone took note of Robert's courage under pressure, high ethical standards, perseverance, curiosity, adaptability, respect for diversity, and team-building skills. Robert suddenly realized that even his small, unconscious behaviors had made a huge impression on others. In many cases, he had forgotten about the specific examples cited until he read the feedback, because his behavior in those situations had felt like second nature to him.

The RBS exercise confirmed Robert's sense of himself, but for those who are unaware of their strengths, the exercise can be truly illuminating. Edward, for example, was a recently minted MBA executive in an automotive firm. His colleagues and subordinates were older and more experienced than he, and he felt uncomfortable disagreeing with them. But he learned through the RBS exercise that his peers appreciated his candid alternative views and respected the diplomatic and respectful manner with which he made his assertions. As a result, Edward grew bolder in making the case for his ideas, knowing that his boss and colleagues listened to him, learned from him, and appreciated what he had to say.

Other times, the RBS exercise sheds a more nuanced light on the skills one takes for granted. Beth, for example, was a lawyer who negotiated on behalf of nonprofit organizations. Throughout her life, Beth had been told she was a good listener, but her exercise respondents noted that the interactive, empathetic, and insightful manner in which she listened made her particularly effective. The specificity of the feedback encouraged Beth to take the lead in future negotiations that required delicate and diplomatic communications.

For naturally analytical people, the analysis portion of the exercise serves both to integrate the feedback and develop a larger picture of their capabilities. Janet, an engineer, thought she could study her feedback as she would a technical drawing of a suspension bridge. She saw her "reflected best self" as something to interrogate and improve. But as she read the remarks from family, friends, and colleagues, she saw herself in a broader and more human context. Over time, the stories she read about her enthusiasm and love of design helped her rethink her career path toward more managerial roles in which she might lead and motivate others.

Step 3: Compose Your Self-Portrait

The next step is to write a description of yourself that summarizes and distills the accumulated information. The description should weave themes from the feedback together with your self-observations into a composite of who you are at your best. The self-portrait is not designed to be a complete psychological and cognitive profile. Rather, it should be an insightful image that you can use as a reminder of your previous contributions and as a guide for future action. The portrait itself should not be a set of bullet points but rather a prose composition beginning with the phrase, "When I am at my best, I . . ." The process of writing out a two- to four-paragraph narrative cements the image of your best self in your consciousness. The narrative form also helps you draw connections between the themes in your life that may previously have seemed disjointed or unrelated. Composing the portrait takes time and demands careful consideration, but at the end of this process, you should come away with a rejuvenated image of who you are.

In developing his self-portrait, Robert drew on the actual words that others used to describe him, rounding out the picture with his own sense of himself at his best. He excised competencies that felt off the mark. This didn't mean he discounted them, but he wanted to assure that the overall portrait felt authentic and powerful. "When I am at my best," Robert wrote,

I stand by my values and can get others to understand why doing so is important. I choose the harder right over the easier wrong. I enjoy setting an example. When I am in learning mode and am curious and passionate about a project, I can work intensely and untiringly. I enjoy taking things on that others might be afraid of or see as too difficult. I'm able to set limits and find alternatives when a current approach is not working. I don't always assume that I am right or know best, which engenders respect from others. I try to empower and give credit to others. I am tolerant and open to differences.

As Robert developed his portrait, he began to understand why he hadn't performed his best at work: He lacked a sense of mission. In the army, he drew satisfaction from the knowledge that the safety of the men and women he led, as well as the nation he served, depended on the quality of his work. He enjoyed the sense of teamwork and variety of problems to be solved. But as an IT manager in charge of routine maintenance on new hardware products, he felt bored and isolated from other people.

The portrait-writing process also helped Robert create a more vivid and elaborate sense of what psychologists would call his "possible self"—not just the person he is in his day-to-day job but the person he might be in completely different contexts. Organizational researchers have shown that when we develop a sense of our best possible self, we are better able to make positive changes in our lives.

Step 4: Redesign Your Job

Having pinpointed his strengths, Robert's next step was to redesign his personal job description to build on what he was good at. Given the fact that routine maintenance work left him cold, Robert's challenge was to create a better fit between his work and his best self. Like most RBS participants, Robert found that the strengths the exercise identified could be put into play in his current position. This involved making small changes in the way he worked, in the composition of his team, and in the way he spent his time. (Most jobs have degrees of freedom in all three of these areas; the trick is operating within the fixed constraints of your job to redesign work at the margins, allowing you to better play to your strengths.)

Robert began by scheduling meetings with systems designers and engineers who told him they were having trouble getting timely information flowing between their groups and Robert's maintenance team. If communication improved, Robert believed, new products would not continue to be saddled with the serious and costly maintenance issues seen in the past. Armed with a carefully documented history of those maintenance problems as well as a new understanding of his naturally analytical and creative team-building skills, Robert began meeting regularly with the designers and engineers to brainstorm better ways to prevent problems with new products. The meetings satisfied two of Robert's deepest best-self needs: He was interacting with more people at work, and he was actively learning about systems design and engineering.

Robert's efforts did not go unnoticed. Key executives remarked on his initiative and his ability to collaborate across functions, as well as on the critical role he played in making new products more reliable. They also saw how he gave credit to others. In less than nine months, Robert's hard work paid off, and he was promoted to program manager. In addition to receiving more pay and higher visibility, Robert enjoyed his work more. His passion was reignited; he felt intensely alive and authentic. Whenever he felt down or lacking in energy, he reread the original e-mail feedback he had received. In difficult situations, the e-mail messages helped him feel more resilient.

Robert was able to leverage his strengths to perform better, but there are cases in which RBS findings conflict with the realities of a person's job. This was true for James, a sales executive who told us he was "in a world of hurt" over his work situation. Unable to meet his ambitious sales goals, tired of flying around the globe to fight fires, his family life on the verge of collapse, James had suffered enough. The RBS exercise revealed that James was at his best when managing people and leading change, but these natural skills did not and could not come into play in his current job. Not long after he did the exercise, he quit his high-stress position and started his own successful company.

Other times, the findings help managers aim for undreamed-of positions in their own organizations. Sarah, a high-level administrator at a university, shared her best-self portrait with key colleagues, asking them to help her identify ways to better exploit her strengths and talents. They suggested that she would be an ideal candidate for a new executive position. Previously, she would never have considered applying for the job, believing herself unqualified. To her surprise, she handily beat out the other candidates.

Beyond Good Enough

We have noted that while people remember criticism, awareness of faults doesn't necessarily translate into better performance. Based on that understanding, the RBS exercise helps you remember your strengths—and construct a plan to build on them. Knowing your strengths also offers you a better understanding of how to deal with your weaknesses—and helps you gain the confidence you need to address them. It allows you to say, "I'm great at leading but lousy at numbers. So rather than teach me remedial math, get me a good finance partner." It also allows you to be clearer in addressing your areas of weakness as a manager. When Tim, a financial services executive, received feedback that he was a great listener and coach, he also became more aware that he had a tendency to spend too much time being a cheerleader and too little time keeping his employees to task. Susan, a senior advertising executive, had the opposite problem: While her feedback lauded her results-oriented management approach, she wanted to be sure that she hadn't missed opportunities to give her employees the space to learn and make mistakes.

In the end, the strength-based orientation of the RBS exercise helps you get past the "good enough" bar. Once you discover who you are at the top of your game, you can use your strengths to better shape the positions you choose to play—both now and in the next phase of your career.

Originally published in January 2005. Reprint R0501G

The Power of Small Wins

Want to truly engage your workers?
Help them see their own progress.

by Teresa M. Amabile and Steven J. Kramer

WHAT IS THE BEST WAY to drive innovative work inside organizations? Important clues hide in the stories of world-renowned creators. It turns out that ordinary scientists, marketers, programmers, and other unsung knowledge workers, whose jobs require creative productivity every day, have more in common with famous innovators than most managers realize. The workday events that ignite their emotions, fuel their motivation, and trigger their perceptions are fundamentally the same.

The Double Helix, James Watson's 1968 memoir about discovering the structure of DNA, describes the roller coaster of emotions he and Francis Crick experienced through the progress and setbacks of the work that eventually earned them the Nobel Prize. After the excitement of their first attempt to build a DNA model, Watson and Crick noticed some serious flaws. According to Watson, "Our first minutes with the models . . . were not joyous." Later that evening, "a shape began to emerge which brought back our spirits." But when they showed their "breakthrough" to colleagues, they found that their model would not work. Dark days of doubt and ebbing motivation followed. When the duo finally had their bona fide breakthrough, and their colleagues found no fault with it, Watson wrote, "My morale skyrocketed, for I suspected that we now had the answer to the riddle." Watson and Crick were so driven by this success that they practically lived in the lab, trying to complete the work.

Throughout these episodes, Watson and Crick's progress—or lack thereof—ruled their reactions. In our recent research on creative work inside businesses, we stumbled upon a remarkably similar phenomenon. Through exhaustive analysis of diaries kept by knowledge workers, we discovered the *progress principle*: Of all the things that can boost emotions, motivation, and perceptions during a workday, the single most important is making progress in meaningful work. And the more frequently people experience that sense of progress, the more likely they are to be creatively productive in the long run. Whether they are trying to solve a major scientific mystery or simply produce a high-quality product or service, everyday progress—even a small win—can make all the difference in how they feel and perform.

The power of progress is fundamental to human nature, but few managers understand it or know how to leverage progress to boost motivation. In fact, work motivation has been a subject of longstanding debate. In a survey asking about the keys to motivating workers, we found that some managers ranked recognition for good work as most important, while others put more stock in tangible incentives. Some focused on the value of interpersonal support, while still others thought clear goals were the answer. Interestingly, very few of our surveyed managers ranked progress first. (See the sidebar "A Surprise for Managers.")

If you are a manager, the progress principle holds clear implications for where to focus your efforts. It suggests that you have more influence than you may realize over employees' well-being, motivation, and creative output. Knowing what serves to catalyze and nourish progress—and what does the opposite—turns out to be the key to effectively managing people and their work.

In this article, we share what we have learned about the power of progress and how managers can leverage it. We spell out how a focus on progress translates into concrete managerial actions and provide a checklist to help make such behaviors habitual. But

Idea in Brief

What is the best way to motivate employees to do creative work? Help them take a step forward every day. In an analysis of knowledge workers' diaries, the authors found that nothing contributed more to a positive inner work life (the mix of emotions, motivations, and perceptions that is critical to performance) than making progress in meaningful work. If a person is motivated and happy at the end of the workday, it's a good bet that he or she achieved something, however small. If the person drags out of the office disengaged and joyless, a setback is likely to blame. This progress principle suggests that managers have more influence than they may realize over employees' well-being, motivation, and creative output.

The key is to learn which actions support progress—such as setting clear goals, providing sufficient time and resources, and offering recognition—and which have the opposite effect. Even small wins can boost inner work life tremendously. On the flip side, small losses or setbacks can have an extremely negative effect. And the work doesn't need to involve curing cancer in order to be meaningful. It simply must matter to the person doing it. The actions that set in motion the positive feedback loop between progress and inner work life may sound like Management 101, but it takes discipline to establish new habits. The authors provide a checklist that managers can use on a daily basis to monitor their progress-enhancing behaviors.

to clarify why those actions are so potent, we first describe our research and what the knowledge workers' diaries revealed about their *inner work lives*.

Inner Work Life and Performance

For nearly 15 years, we have been studying the psychological experiences and the performance of people doing complex work inside organizations. Early on, we realized that a central driver of creative, productive performance was the quality of a person's inner work life—the mix of emotions, motivations, and perceptions over the course of a workday. How happy workers feel; how motivated they are by an intrinsic interest in the work; how positively they view their organization, their management, their team, their work, and

A Surprise for Managers

IN A 1968 ISSUE OF HBR, Frederick Herzberg published a now-classic article titled "One More Time: How Do You Motivate Employees?" Our findings are consistent with his message: People are most satisfied with their jobs (and therefore most motivated) when those jobs give them the opportunity to experience achievement.

The diary research we describe in this article—in which we microscopically examined the events of thousands of workdays, in real time—uncovered the mechanism underlying the sense of achievement: making consistent, meaningful progress.

But managers seem not to have taken Herzberg's lesson to heart. To assess contemporary awareness of the importance of daily work progress, we recently administered a survey to 669 managers of varying levels from dozens of companies around the world. We asked about the managerial tools that can affect employees' motivation and emotions. The respondents ranked five tools—support for making progress in the work, recognition for good work, incentives, interpersonal support, and clear goals—in order of importance.

Fully 95% of the managers who took our survey would probably be surprised to learn that supporting progress is the primary way to elevate motivation—because that's the percentage that failed to rank progress number one. In fact, only 35 managers ranked progress as the number one motivator—a mere 5%. The vast majority of respondents ranked support for making progress dead last as a motivator and third as an influence on emotion. They ranked "recognition for good work (either public or private)" as the most important factor in motivating workers and making them happy. In our diary study, recognition certainly did boost inner work life. But it wasn't nearly as prominent as progress. Besides, without work achievements, there is little to recognize.

---

themselves—all these combine either to push them to higher levels of achievement or to drag them down.

To understand such interior dynamics better, we asked members of project teams to respond individually to an end-of-day e-mail survey during the course of the project—just over four months, on average. (For more on this research, see our article "Inner Work Life: Understanding the Subtext of Business Performance," HBR May 2007.) The projects—inventing kitchen gadgets, managing product lines of cleaning tools, and solving complex IT problems for a hotel empire, for example—all involved creativity. The daily survey inquired about participants' emotions and moods, motivation levels, and perceptions of the work environment that day, as well as what work they did and what events stood out in their minds.

Twenty-six project teams from seven companies participated, comprising 238 individuals. This yielded nearly 12,000 diary entries. Naturally, every individual in our population experienced ups and downs. Our goal was to discover the states of inner work life and the workday events that correlated with the highest levels of creative output.

In a dramatic rebuttal to the commonplace claim that high pressure and fear spur achievement, we found that, at least in the realm of knowledge work, people are more creative and productive when their inner work lives are positive—when they feel happy, are intrinsically motivated by the work itself, and have positive perceptions of their colleagues and the organization. Moreover, in those positive states, people are more committed to the work and more collegial toward those around them. Inner work life, we saw, can fluctuate from one day to the next—sometimes wildly—and performance along with it. A person's inner work life on a given day fuels his or her performance for the day and can even affect performance the *next* day.

Once this *inner work life effect* became clear, our inquiry turned to whether and how managerial action could set it in motion. What events could evoke positive or negative emotions, motivations, and perceptions? The answers were tucked within our research participants' diary entries. There are predictable triggers that inflate or deflate inner work life, and, even accounting for variation among individuals, they are pretty much the same for everyone.

The Power of Progress

Our hunt for inner work life triggers led us to the progress principle. When we compared our research participants' best and worst days (based on their overall mood, specific emotions, and motivation levels), we found that the most common event triggering a "best day" was any progress in the work by the individual or the team. The most common event triggering a "worst day" was a setback.

Consider, for example, how progress relates to one component of inner work life: overall mood ratings. Steps forward occurred on 76% of people's best-mood days. By contrast, setbacks occurred on only 13% of those days. (See the exhibit "What happens on a good day?")

Two other types of inner work life triggers also occur frequently on best days: *Catalysts*, actions that directly support work, including help from a person or group, and *nourishers*, events such as shows of respect and words of encouragement. Each has an opposite: *Inhibitors*, actions that fail to support or actively hinder work, and *toxins*, discouraging or undermining events. Whereas catalysts and inhibitors are directed at the project, nourishers and toxins are directed at the person. Like setbacks, inhibitors and toxins are rare on days of great inner work life.

Events on worst-mood days are nearly the mirror image of those on best-mood days (see the exhibit "What happens on a bad day?").

What happens on a good day?

Progress—even a small step forward—occurs on many of the days people report being in a good mood.

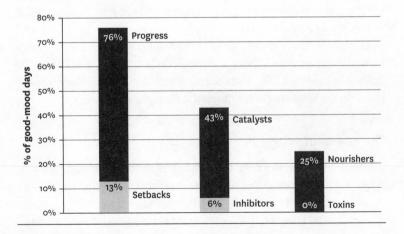

What happens on a bad day?

Events on bad days—setbacks and other hindrances—are nearly the mirror image of those on good days.

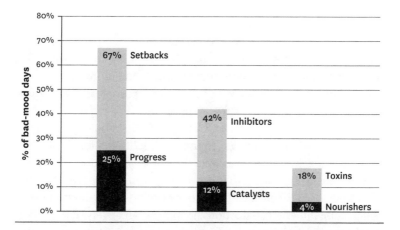

Here, setbacks predominated, occurring on 67% of those days; progress occurred on only 25% of them. Inhibitors and toxins also marked many worst-mood days, and catalysts and nourishers were rare.

This is the progress principle made visible: If a person is motivated and happy at the end of the workday, it's a good bet that he or she made some progress. If the person drags out of the office disengaged and joyless, a setback is most likely to blame.

When we analyzed all 12,000 daily surveys filled out by our participants, we discovered that progress and setbacks influence all three aspects of inner work life. On days when they made progress, our participants reported more positive *emotions*. They not only were in a more upbeat mood in general but also expressed more joy, warmth, and pride. When they suffered setbacks, they experienced more frustration, fear, and sadness.

Motivations were also affected: On progress days, people were more intrinsically motivated—by interest in and enjoyment of the work itself. On setback days, they were not only less intrinsically motivated but also less extrinsically motivated by recognition.

Apparently, setbacks can lead a person to feel generally apathetic and disinclined to do the work at all.

Perceptions differed in many ways, too. On progress days, people perceived significantly more positive challenge in their work. They saw their teams as more mutually supportive and reported more positive interactions between the teams and their supervisors. On a number of dimensions, perceptions suffered when people encountered setbacks. They found less positive challenge in the work, felt that they had less freedom in carrying it out, and reported that they had insufficient resources. On setback days, participants perceived both their teams and their supervisors as less supportive.

To be sure, our analyses establish correlations but do not prove causality. Were these changes in inner work life the result of progress and setbacks, or was the effect the other way around? The numbers alone cannot answer that. However, we do know, from reading thousands of diary entries, that more-positive perceptions, a sense of accomplishment, satisfaction, happiness, and even elation often followed progress. Here's a typical post-progress entry, from a programmer: "I smashed that bug that's been frustrating me for almost a calendar week. That may not be an event to you, but I live a very drab life, so I'm all hyped."

Likewise, we saw that deteriorating perceptions, frustration, sadness, and even disgust often followed setbacks. As another participant, a product marketer, wrote, "We spent a lot of time updating the Cost Reduction project list, and after tallying all the numbers, we are still coming up short of our goal. It is discouraging to not be able to hit it after all the time spent and hard work."

Almost certainly, the causality goes both ways, and managers can use this feedback loop between progress and inner work life to support both.

Minor Milestones

When we think about progress, we often imagine how good it feels to achieve a long-term goal or experience a major breakthrough. These big wins are great—but they are relatively rare. The good news is that even small wins can boost inner work life tremendously. Many of the progress events our research participants reported represented only minor steps forward. Yet they often evoked outsize positive reactions. Consider this diary entry from a programmer in a high-tech company, which was accompanied by very positive self-ratings of her emotions, motivations, and perceptions that day: "I figured out why something was not working correctly. I felt relieved and happy because this was a minor milestone for me."

Even ordinary, incremental progress can increase people's engagement in the work and their happiness during the workday. Across all types of events our participants reported, a notable proportion (28%) of incidents that had a minor impact on the project had a major impact on people's feelings about it. Because inner work life has such a potent effect on creativity and productivity, and because small but consistent steps forward, shared by many people, can accumulate into excellent execution, progress events that often go unnoticed are critical to the overall performance of organizations.

Unfortunately, there is a flip side. Small losses or setbacks can have an extremely negative effect on inner work life. In fact, our study and research by others show that negative events can have a more powerful impact than positive ones. Consequently, it is especially important for managers to minimize daily hassles.

Progress in Meaningful Work

We've shown how gratifying it is for workers when they are able to chip away at a goal, but recall what we said earlier: The key to motivating performance is supporting progress in *meaningful* work. Making headway boosts your inner work life, but only if the work matters to you.

Think of the most boring job you've ever had. Many people nominate their first job as a teenager—washing pots and pans in a restaurant kitchen, for example, or checking coats at a museum. In jobs like those, the power of progress seems elusive. No matter how hard you work, there are always more pots to wash and coats to check; only punching the time clock at the end of the day or getting the paycheck at the end of the week yields a sense of accomplishment.

In jobs with much more challenge and room for creativity, like the ones our research participants had, simply "making progress"— getting tasks done—doesn't guarantee a good inner work life, either. You may have experienced this rude fact in your own job, on days (or in projects) when you felt demotivated, devalued, and frustrated, even though you worked hard and got things done. The likely cause is your perception of the completed tasks as peripheral or irrelevant. For the progress principle to operate, the work must be meaningful to the person doing it.

In 1983, Steve Jobs was trying to entice John Sculley to leave a wildly successful career at PepsiCo to become Apple's new CEO. Jobs reportedly asked him, "Do you want to spend the rest of your life selling sugared water or do you want a chance to change the world?" In making his pitch, Jobs leveraged a potent psychological force: the deep-seated human desire to do meaningful work.

Fortunately, to feel meaningful, work doesn't have to involve putting the first personal computers in the hands of ordinary people, or alleviating poverty, or helping to cure cancer. Work with less profound importance to society can matter if it contributes value to something or someone important to the worker. Meaning can be as simple as making a useful and high-quality product for a customer or providing a genuine service for a community. It can be supporting a colleague or boosting an organization's profits by reducing inefficiencies in a production process. Whether the goals are lofty or modest, as long as they are meaningful to the worker and it is clear how his or her efforts contribute to them, progress toward them can galvanize inner work life.

In principle, managers shouldn't have to go to extraordinary lengths to infuse jobs with meaning. Most jobs in modern organizations are potentially meaningful for the people doing them. However, managers can make sure that employees know just how their work is contributing. And, most important, they can avoid actions that negate its value. (See the sidebar "How Work Gets Stripped of Its

Meaning.") All the participants in our research were doing work that should have been meaningful; no one was washing pots or checking coats. Shockingly often, however, we saw potentially important, challenging work losing its power to inspire.

Supporting Progress: Catalysts and Nourishers

What can managers do to ensure that people are motivated, committed, and happy? How can they support workers' daily progress? They can use catalysts and nourishers, the other kinds of frequent "best day" events we discovered.

Catalysts are actions that support work. They include setting clear goals, allowing autonomy, providing sufficient resources and time, helping with the work, openly learning from problems and successes, and allowing a free exchange of ideas. Their opposites, inhibitors, include failing to provide support and actively interfering with the work. Because of their impact on progress, catalysts and inhibitors ultimately affect inner work life. But they also have a more immediate impact: When people realize that they have clear and meaningful goals, sufficient resources, helpful colleagues, and so on, they get an instant boost to their emotions, their motivation to do a great job, and their perceptions of the work and the organization.

Nourishers are acts of interpersonal support, such as respect and recognition, encouragement, emotional comfort, and opportunities for affiliation. Toxins, their opposites, include disrespect, discouragement, disregard for emotions, and interpersonal conflict. For good and for ill, nourishers and toxins affect inner work life directly and immediately.

Catalysts and nourishers—and their opposites—can alter the meaningfulness of work by shifting people's perceptions of their jobs and even themselves. For instance, when a manager makes sure that people have the resources they need, it signals to them that what they are doing is important and valuable. When managers recognize people for the work they do, it signals that they are important to the organization. In this way, catalysts and nourishers

How Work Gets Stripped of Its Meaning

DIARY ENTRIES FROM 238 knowledge workers who were members of creative project teams revealed four primary ways in which managers unwittingly drain work of its meaning.

1. Managers may dismiss the importance of employees' work or ideas. Consider the case of Richard, a senior lab technician at a chemical company, who found meaning in helping his new-product development team solve complex technical problems. However, in team meetings over the course of a three-week period, Richard perceived that his team leader was ignoring his suggestions and those of his teammates. As a result, he felt that his contributions were not meaningful, and his spirits flagged. When at last he believed that he was again making a substantive contribution to the success of the project, his mood improved dramatically:

   > I felt much better at today's team meeting. I felt that my opinions and information were important to the project and that we have made some progress.

2. They may destroy employees' sense of ownership of their work. Frequent and abrupt reassignments often have this effect. This happened repeatedly to the members of a product development team in a giant consumer products company, as described by team member Bruce:

   > As I've been handing over some projects, I do realize that I don't like to give them up. Especially when you have been with them from the

---

can lend greater meaning to the work—and amplify the operation of the progress principle.

The managerial actions that constitute catalysts and nourishers are not particularly mysterious; they may sound like Management 101, if not just common sense and common decency. But our diary study reminded us how often they are ignored or forgotten. Even some of the more attentive managers in the companies we studied did not consistently provide catalysts and nourishers. For example, a supply-chain specialist named Michael was, in many ways and on most days, an excellent subteam manager. But he was occasionally so overwhelmed that he became toxic toward his people. When a supplier failed to complete a "hot" order on time and Michael's team had to resort to air shipping to meet the customer's deadline, he realized that the profit margin on the sale would be blown. In irritation,

start and are nearly to the end. You lose ownership. This happens to us way too often.

3. Managers may send the message that the work employees are doing will never see the light of day. They can signal this—unintentionally—by shifting their priorities or changing their minds about how something should be done. We saw the latter in an internet technology company after user-interface developer Burt had spent weeks designing seamless transitions for non-English-speaking users. Not surprisingly, Burt's mood was seriously marred on the day he reported this incident:

> Other options for the international [interfaces] were [given] to the team during a team meeting, which could render the work I am doing useless.

4. They may neglect to inform employees about unexpected changes in a customer's priorities. Often, this arises from poor customer management or inadequate communication within the company. For example, Stuart, a data transformation expert at an IT company, reported deep frustration and low motivation on the day he learned that weeks of the team's hard work might have been for naught:

> Found out that there is a strong possibility that the project may not be going forward, due to a shift in the client's agenda. Therefore, there is a strong possibility that all the time and effort put into the project was a waste of our time.

he lashed out at his subordinates, demeaning the solid work they had done and disregarding their own frustration with the supplier. In his diary, he admitted as much:

> As of Friday, we have spent $28,000 in air freight to send 1,500 $30 spray jet mops to our number two customer. Another 2,800 remain on this order, and there is a good probability that they too will gain wings. I have turned from the kindly Supply Chain Manager into the black-masked executioner. All similarity to civility is gone, our backs are against the wall, flight is not possible, therefore fight is probable.

Even when managers don't have their backs against the wall, developing long-term strategy and launching new initiatives can often seem more important—and perhaps sexier—than making sure that subordinates have what they need to make steady progress and feel supported as human beings. But as we saw repeatedly in our research, even the best strategy will fail if managers ignore the people working in the trenches to execute it.

A Model Manager—and a Tool for Emulating Him

We could explain the many (and largely unsurprising) moves that can catalyze progress and nourish spirits, but it may be more useful to give an example of a manager who consistently used those moves—and then to provide a simple tool that can help any manager do so.

Our model manager is Graham, whom we observed leading a small team of chemical engineers within a multinational European firm we'll call Kruger-Bern. The mission of the team's NewPoly project was clear and meaningful enough: develop a safe, biodegradable polymer to replace petrochemicals in cosmetics and, eventually, in a wide range of consumer products. As in many large firms, however, the project was nested in a confusing and sometimes threatening corporate setting of shifting top-management priorities, conflicting signals, and wavering commitments. Resources were uncomfortably tight, and uncertainty loomed over the project's future—and every team member's career. Even worse, an incident early in the project, in which an important customer reacted angrily to a sample, left the team reeling. Yet Graham was able to sustain team members' inner work lives by repeatedly and visibly removing obstacles, materially supporting progress, and emotionally supporting the team.

Graham's management approach excelled in four ways. First, he established a positive climate, one event at a time, which set behavioral norms for the entire team. When the customer complaint stopped the project in its tracks, for example, he engaged immediately with the team to analyze the problem, without recriminations, and develop a plan for repairing the relationship. In doing so, he modeled how to respond to crises in the work: not by panicking or pointing fingers but by identifying problems and their causes, and developing a coordinated action plan. This is both a practical approach and a great way to give subordinates a sense of forward movement even in the face of the missteps and failures inherent in any complex project.

Second, Graham stayed attuned to his team's everyday activities and progress. In fact, the nonjudgmental climate he had established made this happen naturally. Team members updated him frequently—without being asked—on their setbacks, progress, and plans. At one point, one of his hardest-working colleagues, Brady, had to abort a trial of a new material because he couldn't get the parameters right on the equipment. It was bad news, because the NewPoly team had access to the equipment only one day a week, but Brady immediately informed Graham. In his diary entry that evening, Brady noted, "He didn't like the lost week but seemed to understand." That understanding assured Graham's place in the stream of information that would allow him to give his people just what they needed to make progress.

Third, Graham targeted his support according to recent events in the team and the project. Each day, he could anticipate what type of intervention—a catalyst or the removal of an inhibitor; a nourisher or some antidote to a toxin—would have the most impact on team members' inner work lives and progress. And if he could not make that judgment, he asked. Most days it was not hard to figure out, as on the day he received some uplifting news about his bosses' commitment to the project. He knew the team was jittery about a rumored corporate reorganization and could use the encouragement. Even though the clarification came during a well-earned vacation day, he immediately got on the phone to relay the good news to the team.

Finally, Graham established himself as a resource for team members, rather than a micromanager; he was sure to *check in* while never seeming to *check up* on them. Superficially, checking in and checking up seem quite similar, but micromanagers make four kinds of mistakes. First, they fail to allow autonomy in carrying out the work. Unlike Graham, who gave the NewPoly team a clear strategic goal but respected members' ideas about how to meet it, micromanagers dictate every move. Second, they frequently ask subordinates about

The Daily Progress Checklist

Near the end of each workday, use this checklist to review the day and plan your managerial actions for the next day. After a few days, you will be able to identify issues by scanning the boldface words. First, focus on progress and setbacks and think about specific events (catalysts, nourishers, inhibitors, and toxins) that contributed to them. Next, consider any clear inner-work-life clues and what further information they provide about progress and other events. Finally, prioritize for action. The action plan for the next day is the most important part of your daily review: What is the one thing you can do to best facilitate progress?

Progress

Which 1 or 2 events today indicated either a small win or a possible breakthrough? (Describe briefly.)

_____

_____

Catalysts

☐ Did the team have clear short- and long-term **goals** for meaningful work?

☐ Did team members have sufficient **autonomy** to solve problems and take ownership of the project?

☐ Did they have all the **resources** they needed to move forward efficiently?

☐ Did they have sufficient **time** to focus on meaningful work?

☐ Did I give or get them **help** when they needed or requested it? Did I encourage team members to help one another?

☐ Did I discuss **lessons** from today's successes and problems with my team?

☐ Did I help **ideas** flow freely within the group?

Setbacks

Which 1 or 2 events today indicated either a small setback or a possible crisis? (Describe briefly.)

_____

_____

Inhibitors

☐ Was there any confusion regarding long- or short-term **goals** for meaningful work?

☐ Were team members overly **constrained** in their ability to solve problems and feel ownership of the project?

☐ Did they lack any of the **resources** they needed to move forward effectively?

☐ Did they lack sufficient **time** to focus on meaningful work?

☐ Did I or others fail to provide needed or requested **help**?

☐ Did I "punish" failure or neglect to find **lessons** and/ or opportunities in problems and successes?

☐ Did I or others cut off the presentation or debate of **ideas** prematurely?

Nourishers

- ☐ Did I show **respect** to team members by recognizing their contributions to progress, attending to their ideas, and treating them as trusted professionals?

- ☐ Did I **encourage** team members who faced difficult challenges?

- ☐ Did I **support** team members who had a personal or professional problem?

- ☐ Is there a sense of personal and professional **affiliation** and camaraderie within the team?

Toxins

- ☐ Did I **disrespect** any team members by failing to recognize their contributions to progress, not attending to their ideas, or not treating them as trusted professionals?

- ☐ Did I **discourage** a member of the team in any way?

- ☐ Did I **neglect** a team member who had a personal or professional problem?

- ☐ Is there tension or **antagonism** among members of the team or between team members and me?

Inner Work Life

Did I see any indications of the quality of my subordinates' inner work lives today?

Perceptions of the work, team, management, firm _____

Emotions _____

Motivation _____

What specific events might have affected inner work life today? _____

Action Plan

What can I do tomorrow to start eliminating the inhibitors and toxins identified?

What can I do tomorrow to strengthen the catalysts and nourishers identified and provide the ones that are lacking?

_____

_____

_____

_____

their work without providing any real help. By contrast, when one of Graham's team members reported problems, Graham helped analyze them—remaining open to alternative interpretations—and often ended up helping to get things back on track. Third, micromanagers are quick to affix personal blame when problems arise, leading subordinates to hide problems rather than honestly discuss how to surmount them, as Graham did with Brady. And fourth, micromanagers tend to hoard information to use as a secret weapon. Few realize how damaging this is to inner work life. When subordinates perceive that a manager is withholding potentially useful information, they feel infantilized, their motivation wanes, and their work is handicapped. Graham was quick to communicate upper management's views of the project, customers' opinions and needs, and possible sources of assistance or resistance within and outside the organization.

In all those ways, Graham sustained his team's positive emotions, intrinsic motivation, and favorable perceptions. His actions serve as a powerful example of how managers at any level can approach each day determined to foster progress.

We know that many managers, however well-intentioned, will find it hard to establish the habits that seemed to come so naturally to Graham. Awareness, of course, is the first step. However, turning an awareness of the importance of inner work life into routine action takes discipline. With that in mind, we developed a checklist for managers to consult on a daily basis (see the sidebar "The Daily Progress Checklist"). The aim of the checklist is managing for meaningful progress, one day at a time.

The Progress Loop

Inner work life drives performance; in turn, good performance, which depends on consistent progress, enhances inner work life. We call this the *progress loop*; it reveals the potential for self-reinforcing benefits.

So, the most important implication of the progress principle is this: By supporting people and their daily progress in meaningful work, managers improve not only the inner work lives of their employees but also the organization's long-term performance, which enhances inner work life even more. Of course, there is a dark side—the possibility of negative feedback loops. If managers fail to support progress and the people trying to make it, inner work life suffers and so does performance; and degraded performance further undermines inner work life.

A second implication of the progress principle is that managers needn't fret about trying to read the psyches of their workers, or manipulate complicated incentive schemes, to ensure that employees are motivated and happy. As long as they show basic respect and consideration, they can focus on supporting the work itself.

To become an effective manager, you must learn to set this positive feedback loop in motion. That may require a significant shift. Business schools, business books, and managers themselves usually focus on managing organizations or people. But if you focus on managing progress, the management of people—and even of entire organizations—becomes much more feasible. You won't have to figure out how to x-ray the inner work lives of subordinates; if you facilitate their steady progress in meaningful work, make that progress salient to them, and treat them well, they will experience the emotions, motivations, and perceptions necessary for great performance. Their superior work will contribute to organizational success. And here's the beauty of it: They will love their jobs.

Originally published in May 2011. Reprint R1105C

Nine Things Successful People Do Differently

by Heidi Grant

WHY HAVE YOU BEEN SO successful in reaching some of your goals, but not others? If you aren't sure, you are far from alone in your confusion. It turns out that even brilliant, highly accomplished people are pretty lousy when it comes to understanding why they succeed or fail. The intuitive answer—that you are born predisposed to certain talents and lacking in others—is really just one small piece of the puzzle. In fact, decades of research on achievement suggests that successful people reach their goals not simply because of who they are, but more often because of what they do.

1. Get Specific

When you set yourself a goal, try to be as specific as possible. "Lose 5 pounds" is a better goal than "lose some weight," because it gives you a clear idea of what success looks like. Knowing exactly what you want to achieve keeps you motivated until you get there. Also, think about the specific actions that need to be taken to reach your goal. Just promising you'll "eat less" or "sleep more" is too vague— be clear and precise. "I'll be in bed by 10 on weeknights" leaves no room for doubt about what you need to do, and whether or not you've actually done it.

2. Seize the Moment to Act on Your Goals

Given how busy most of us are, and how many goals we are juggling at once, it's not surprising that we routinely miss opportunities to act on a goal because we simply fail to notice them. Did you really have no time to work out today? No chance at any point to return that phone call? Achieving your goal means grabbing hold of these opportunities before they slip through your fingers.

To seize the moment, decide when and where you will take each action you want to take, in advance. Again, be as specific as possible (e.g., "If it's Monday, Wednesday, or Friday, I'll work out for 30 minutes before work.") Studies show that this kind of planning will help your brain to detect and seize the opportunity when it arises, increasing your chances of success by roughly 300 percent.

3. Know Exactly How Far You Have Left to Go

Achieving any goal also requires honest and regular monitoring of your progress—if not by others, then by you yourself. If you don't know how well you are doing, you can't adjust your behavior or your strategies accordingly. Check your progress frequently—weekly, or even daily, depending on the goal.

4. Be a Realistic Optimist

When you are setting a goal, by all means engage in lots of positive thinking about how likely you are to achieve it. Believing in your ability to succeed is enormously helpful for creating and sustaining your motivation. But whatever you do, don't underestimate how difficult it will be to reach your goal. Most goals worth achieving require time, planning, effort, and persistence. Studies show that thinking things will come to you easily and effortlessly leaves you ill-prepared for the journey ahead, and significantly increases the odds of failure.

5. Focus on Getting Better, Rather Than Being Good

Believing you have the ability to reach your goals is important, but so is believing you can get the ability. Many of us believe that our intelligence, our personality, and our physical aptitudes are fixed— that no matter what we do, we won't improve. As a result, we focus on goals that are all about proving ourselves, rather than developing and acquiring new skills.

Fortunately, decades of research suggest that the belief in fixed ability is completely wrong—abilities of all kinds are profoundly malleable. Embracing the fact that you can change will allow you to make better choices, and reach your fullest potential. People whose goals are about getting better, rather than about being good, take difficulty in stride and appreciate the journey as much as the destination.

6. Have Grit

Grit is a willingness to commit to long-term goals and to persist in the face of difficulty. Studies show that gritty people obtain more education in their lifetime and earn higher college GPAs. Grit predicts which cadets will stick out their first grueling year at West Point. In fact, grit even predicts which round contestants will make it to at the Scripps National Spelling Bee.

The good news is, if you aren't particularly gritty now, there is something you can do about it. People who lack grit more often than not believe that they just don't have the innate abilities successful people have. If that describes your own thinking . . . well, there's no way to put this nicely: You are wrong. As I mentioned earlier, effort, planning, persistence, and good strategies are what it really takes to succeed. Embracing this knowledge will not only help you see yourself and your goals more accurately, but also do wonders for your grit.

7. Build Your Willpower Muscle

Your self-control "muscle" is just like the other muscles in your body—when it doesn't get much exercise, it becomes weaker over time. But when you give it regular workouts by putting it to good use, it will grow stronger and stronger, and better able to help you successfully reach your goals.

To build willpower, take on a challenge that requires you to do something you'd honestly rather not do. Give up high-fat snacks, do 100 sit-ups a day, stand up straight when you catch yourself slouching, try to learn a new skill. When you find yourself wanting to give in, give up, or just not bother—don't. Start with just one activity, and make a plan for how you will deal with troubles when they occur ("If I have a craving for a snack, I will eat one piece of fresh or three pieces of dried fruit.") It will be hard in the beginning, but it will get easier, and that's the whole point. As your strength grows, you can take on more challenges and step up your self-control workout.

8. Don't Tempt Fate

No matter how strong your willpower muscle becomes, it's important to always respect the fact that it is limited, and if you overtax it you will temporarily run out of steam. Don't try to take on two challenging tasks at once, if you can help it (like quitting smoking and dieting at the same time). And don't put yourself in harm's way—many people are overly confident in their ability to resist temptation, and as a result they put themselves in situations where temptations abound. Successful people know not to make reaching a goal harder than it already is.

9. Focus on What You Will Do, Not What You Won't Do

Do you want to successfully lose weight, quit smoking, or put a lid on your bad temper? Then plan how you will replace bad habits with good ones, rather than focusing only on the bad habits themselves. Research on thought suppression (e.g., "Don't think about white bears!") has shown that trying to avoid a thought makes it even more active in your mind. The same holds true when it comes to behavior—by trying not to engage in a bad habit, our habits get strengthened rather than broken.

If you want to change your ways, ask yourself, What will I do instead? For example, if you are trying to gain control of your temper and stop flying off the handle, you might make a plan like "If I am starting to feel angry, then I will take three deep breaths to calm down." By using deep breathing as a replacement for giving in to your anger, your bad habit will get worn away over time until it disappears completely.

It is my hope that, after reading about the nine things successful people do differently, you have gained some insight into all the things you have been doing right all along. Even more important, I hope are able to identify the mistakes that have derailed you, and use that knowledge to your advantage from now on. Remember, you don't need to become a different person to become a more successful one. It's never what you are, but what you do.

Originally published February 25, 2011. Reprint H006W2

Make Time for the Work That Matters

by Julian Birkinshaw and Jordan Cohen

MORE HOURS IN THE DAY. It's one thing everyone wants, and yet it's impossible to attain. But what if you could free up significant time—maybe as much as 20% of your workday—to focus on the responsibilities that really matter?

We've spent the past three years studying how knowledge workers can become more productive and found that the answer is simple: Eliminate or delegate unimportant tasks and replace them with value-added ones. Our research indicates that knowledge workers spend a great deal of their time—an average of 41%—on discretionary activities that offer little personal satisfaction and could be handled competently by others. So why do they keep doing them? Because ridding oneself of work is easier said than done. We instinctively cling to tasks that make us feel busy and thus important, while our bosses, constantly striving to do more with less, pile on as many responsibilities as we're willing to accept.

We believe there's a way forward, however. Knowledge workers can make themselves more productive by thinking consciously about how they spend their time; deciding which tasks matter most to them and their organizations; and dropping or creatively outsourcing the rest. We tried this intervention with 15 executives at different companies, and they were able to dramatically reduce their involvement in low-value tasks: They cut desk work by an average of six hours a week and meeting time by an average of two hours a week. And the benefits were clear. For example, when Lotta Laitinen, a manager at

If, a Scandinavian insurance broker, jettisoned meetings and administrative tasks in order to spend more time supporting her team, it led to a 5% increase in sales by her unit over a three-week period.

While not everyone in our study was quite that successful, the results still astounded us. By simply asking knowledge workers to rethink and shift the balance of their work, we were able to help them free up nearly a fifth of their time—an average of one full day a week—and focus on more worthwhile tasks with the hours they saved.

Why It's So Hard

Knowledge workers present a real challenge to managers. The work they do is difficult to observe (since a lot of it happens inside their heads), and the quality of it is frequently subjective. A manager may suspect that an employee is spending her time inefficiently but be hard-pressed to diagnose the problem, let alone come up with a solution.

We interviewed 45 knowledge workers in 39 companies across eight industries in the United States and Europe to see how they spent their days. We found that even the most dedicated and impressive performers devoted large amounts of time to tedious, non-value-added activities such as desk work and "managing across" the organization (for example, meetings with people in other departments). These are tasks that the knowledge workers themselves rated as offering little personal utility and low value to the company.

There are many reasons why this happens. Most of us feel entangled in a web of commitments from which it can be painful to extricate ourselves: We worry that we're letting our colleagues or employers down if we stop doing certain tasks. "I want to appear busy and productive—the company values team players," one participant observed. Also, those less important items on our to-do lists are not entirely without benefit. Making progress on any task—even an inessential one—increases our feelings of engagement and satisfaction, research has shown. And although meetings are widely derided as a waste of time, they offer opportunities to socialize and connect with coworkers. "I actually quite look forward to face-to-face meetings," one respondent told us. "A call is more efficient, but it's a cold, lifeless medium."

Idea in Brief

More hours in the day. It's one thing everyone wants, and yet it's impossible to attain. But what if you could free up significant time—maybe as much as 20% of your workday—to focus on the responsibilities that really matter? The authors' research shows that knowledge workers spend, on average, 41% of their time on activities that offer little personal satisfaction and could be handled competently by others.

Knowledge workers can become more productive by thinking consciously about how they spend their time, deciding which tasks matter most to them and their organizations, and dropping or creatively outsourcing the rest.

The tasks to be dropped are sorted into:

- **quick kills** (things you can stop doing now, without any negative effects)

- **off-load opportunities** (work that can be delegated with minimal effort)

- **long-term redesign** (work that needs to be reconceived or restructured)

Once the tasks are disposed of, the freed-up time is spent focusing on more-important work.

When 15 executives tried this, they were able to reduce desk work by an average of six hours per week and meetings by two hours per week. They filled the time with value-added tasks like coaching and strategizing.

Organizations share some of the blame for less-than-optimal productivity. Cost cutting has been prevalent over the past decade, and knowledge workers, like most employees, have had to take on some low-value tasks—such as making travel arrangements—that distract them from more important work. Even though business confidence is rebounding, many companies are hesitant to add back resources, particularly administrative ones. What's more, increasingly complicated regulatory environments and tighter control systems in many industries have contributed to risk-averse corporate cultures that discourage senior people from ceding work to less seasoned colleagues. The consequences are predictable: "My team is understaffed and underskilled, so my calendar is a nightmare and I get pulled into many more meetings than I should," one study subject reported. Another commented, "I face the constraint of the working capacity of the people I delegate to."

The work that knowledge workers do

Our research shows that desk-based work and "managing across" take up two-thirds of knowledge workers' time, on average . . .

Time spent on activities

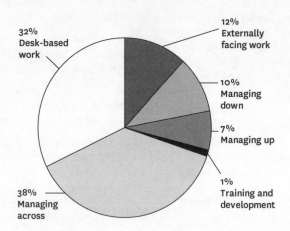

32% Desk-based work

12% Externally facing work

10% Managing down

7% Managing up

1% Training and development

38% Managing across

. . . and yet those tasks were rated as most easily off-loaded and tiresome.

Worth the time?

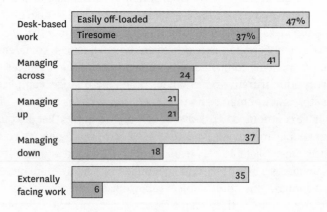

Desk-based work — Easily off-loaded 47%, Tiresome 37%

Managing across — 41, 24

Managing up — 21, 21

Managing down — 37, 18

Externally facing work — 35, 6

Armed with this knowledge, study participants dropped, delegated, outsourced, or postponed low-value tasks to free up time for more important work.

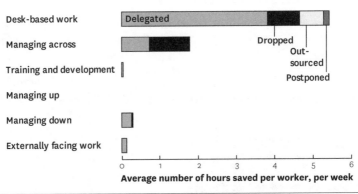

Some companies do try to help their knowledge workers focus on the value-added parts of their job. For example, one of us (Jordan Cohen) helped Pfizer create a service called pfizerWorks, which allows employees to outsource less important tasks. We've also seen corporate initiatives that ban e-mail on Fridays, put time limits on meetings, and forbid internal PowerPoint presentations. But it's very difficult to change institutional norms, and when knowledge workers don't buy in to such top-down directives, they find creative ways to resist or game the system, which only makes matters worse. We propose a sensible middle ground: judicious, self-directed interventions supported by management that help knowledge workers help themselves.

What Workers Can Do

Our process, a variant of the classic Start/Stop/Continue exercise, is designed to help you make small but significant changes to your day-to-day work schedule. We facilitated this exercise with the 15 executives mentioned above, and they achieved some remarkable results.

Self-Assessment:
Identifying Low-Value Tasks

MAKE A LIST OF EVERYTHING YOU DID yesterday or the day before, divided into 30- or 60-minute chunks. For each task, ask yourself four questions:

How valuable is this activity to the firm?

Suppose you're updating your boss or a senior executive on your performance. Would you mention this task? Would you be able to justify spending time on it?

	Score
It contributes in a significant way toward the company's overall objectives	4
It contributes in a small way	3
It has no impact, positive or negative	2
It has a negative impact	1

To what extent could I let this go?

Imagine that because of a family emergency, you arrive at work two hours late and have to prioritize the day's activities. Which category would this activity fall in?

Essential: This takes top priority	4
Important: I need to get this done today	3
Discretionary: I'll get to it if time allows	2
Unimportant/optional: I can cut this immediately	1

How much personal value do I get from doing it?

Imagine that you're financially independent and creating your dream job. Would you keep this task or jettison it?

Identify low-value tasks

Using our self-assessment, look at all your daily activities and decide which ones are (a) not that important to either you or your firm and (b) relatively easy to drop, delegate, or outsource. Our research suggests that at least one-quarter of a typical knowledge worker's

Definitely keep: It's one of the best parts of my job	5
Probably keep: I enjoy this activity	4
Not sure: This task has good and bad points	3
Probably drop: I find this activity somewhat tiresome	2
Definitely jettison: I dislike doing it	1

To what extent could someone else do it on my behalf?

Suppose you've been tapped to handle a critical, fast-track initiative and have to assign some of your work to colleagues for three months. Would you drop, delegate, or keep this task?

Only I (or someone senior to me) can handle this task	5
This task is best done by me because of my particular skill set and other, linked responsibilities	4
If structured properly, this task could be handled satisfactorily by someone junior to me	3
This task could easily be handled by a junior employee or outsourced to a third party	2
This task could be dropped altogether	1

Tally your score

A low total score (10 or lower) reflects a task that is a likely candidate for delegation or elimination.

To see how you stack up and to get advice for improved productivity, go to hbr.org/web/2013/08/assessment/make-time-for-work-that-matters for an interactive assessment tool.

activities fall into both categories, so you should aim to find up to 10 hours of time per week. The participants in our study pinpointed a range of expendable tasks. Lotta Laitinen, the manager at If, quickly identified several meetings and routine administrative tasks she could dispense with. Shantanu Kumar, CEO of a small technology company in London, realized he was too involved in project planning details, while Vincent Bryant, a manager at GDF SUEZ Energy Services, was surprised to see how much time he was wasting in sorting documents.

Decide whether to drop, delegate, or redesign

Sort the low-value tasks into three categories: *quick kills* (things you can stop doing now with no negative effects), *off-load opportunities* (tasks that can be delegated with minimal effort), and *long-term redesign* (work that needs to be restructured or overhauled). Our study participants found that this step forced them to reflect carefully on their real contributions to their respective organizations. "I took a step back and asked myself, 'Should I be doing this in the first place? Can my subordinate do it? Is he up to it?'" recalls Johann Barchechath, a manager at BNP Paribas. "This helped me figure out what was valuable for the bank versus what was valuable for me—and what we simply shouldn't have been doing at all." Another participant noted, "I realized that the big change I should make is to say no up-front to low-value tasks and not commit myself in the first place."

Off-load tasks

We heard from many participants that delegation was initially the most challenging part—but ultimately very rewarding. One participant said he couldn't stop worrying about the tasks he had reassigned, while another told us he had trouble remembering "to push, prod, and chase." Barchechath observed, "I learned about the importance of timing in delegating something—it is possible to delegate too early."

Most participants eventually overcame those stumbling blocks. They delegated from 2% to 20% of their work with no decline in their productivity or their team's. "I overestimated my subordinate's capability at first, but it got easier after a while, and even having a partially done piece of work created energy for me," Barchechath said. A bonus was that junior employees benefited from getting more involved. "[She] told me several times that she really appreciated it," he added. Vincent Bryant decided to off-load tasks to a virtual personal assistant and says that although he was concerned about getting up to speed with the service, "it was seamless."

Allocate freed-up time

The goal, of course, is to be not just efficient but effective. So the next step is to determine how to best make use of the time you've saved. Write down two or three things you should be doing but aren't, and then keep a log to assess whether you're using your time more effectively. Some of our study participants were able to go home a bit earlier to enjoy their families (which probably made them happier and more productive the next day). Some unfortunately reported that their time was immediately swallowed up by unforeseen events: "I cleared my in-box and found myself firefighting."

But more than half reclaimed the extra hours to do better work. "For me the most useful part was identifying the important things I don't get time for usually," Kumar said. "I stopped spending time with my project planning tool and instead focused on strategic activities, such as the product road map." Laitinen used her freed-up schedule to listen in on client calls, observe her top salespeople, and coach her employees one-on-one. The result was that stunning three-week sales jump of 5%, with the biggest increases coming from below-average performers. A questionnaire showed that employee responses to the experiment were positive, and Laitinen found that she missed nothing by dropping some of her work. "The first week was really stressful, because I had to do so much planning, but by the middle of the test period, I was more relaxed, and I was satisfied when I went home every day."

Commit to your plan

Although this process is entirely self-directed, it's crucial to share your plan with a boss, colleague, or mentor. Explain which activities you are getting out of and why. And agree to discuss what you've achieved in a few weeks' time. Without this step, it's all too easy to slide back into bad habits. Many of our participants found that their managers were helpful and supportive. Laitinen's boss, Sven Kärnekull, suggested people to whom she could delegate her work.

Other participants discovered that simply voicing the commitment to another person helped them follow through.

With relatively little effort and no management directive, the small intervention we propose can significantly boost productivity among knowledge workers. Such shifts are not always easy, of course. "It's hard to make these changes without the discipline of someone standing over you," one of our study participants remarked. But all agreed that the exercise was a useful "forcing mechanism" to help them become more efficient, effective, and engaged employees and managers. To do the same, you don't have to redesign any parts of an organization, reengineer a work process, or transform a business model. All you have to do is ask the right questions and act on the answers. After all, if you're a knowledge worker, isn't using your judgment what you were hired for?

Originally published in September 2013. Reprint R1309K

Don't Be Blinded by Your Own Expertise

by Sydney Finkelstein

EXPERTISE SOUNDS LIKE an unqualified good in professional contexts. Companies associate it with high performance and leadership capability and seek it when hiring for key roles. But in studying top executives over the past decade, I've come to understand that expertise can also severely *impede* performance, in two important ways.

Consider the case of Matthew Broderick, who led the Homeland Security Operations Center when Hurricane Katrina slammed into New Orleans, in August 2005. A brigadier general with 30 years' experience running emergency operations, including a stint at the helm of the U.S. Marine Corps National Command Center, he seemed like the perfect person to oversee the response to the storm. "Been there, done that," he said when describing his qualifications for the role.

Yet Broderick didn't trigger key elements of the rescue-and-relief efforts until more than a day after Katrina hit. He underestimated the extent of the catastrophe with tragic consequences, owing in part to his expert mindset, which prevented him from appreciating that adept as he was at handling crises in military contexts, he had little experience with natural disasters in the civilian realm. Trained to verify every fact, thereby avoiding decisions made in the "fog of war," he failed to recognize that in this case speed was more important. He relied too heavily on military intelligence instead of trusting local or state sources. And because of his extensive Marine Corps expertise, he assumed—wrongly—that key federal emergency officials would automatically report information up the chain of command. He seems to have believed that his brilliance in one area would render him competent in another.

This type of overconfidence is one form of what I call *the expertise trap.* Another is when leaders' deep knowledge and experience leaves them incurious, blinkered, and vulnerable—even in their own fields. Motorola executives in the 1990s became so obsessed with the Six Sigma continuous improvement methodology, in which they had developed considerable expertise, that they missed the significance of the industry's shift to digital technologies and fell dramatically behind their competitors. A decade or so later, when Apple first released its iPhone, technology experts were quick to call it a failure, with then Microsoft CEO Steve Ballmer, who'd been steeped in the company's PC and connected computing business, proclaiming that a device without the traditional QWERTY keypad had no chance of garnering significant market share. More recently, large retailers have struggled to compete with Amazon because senior executives have relied too much on their established expertise as merchandisers and on familiar tactics such as store design, closures, and alterations to the marketing mix. In each of these cases experts assumed that what they knew was right and always would be. As reality shifted, that closed-mindedness led to poor execution and subpar results.

When we begin to identify as experts, our outlook can narrow, both in daily work and in times of crisis. We become reluctant to admit mistakes and failings, thus hindering our development. We distance ourselves from those "beneath" us, making it harder to earn their affection and trust. And as the dynamics of our businesses change, we risk being bypassed or replaced by colleagues on the rise, outsiders adept at learning new things, or artificial intelligence algorithms that can perform rote tasks faster and better than we can. Over time the very expertise that led to our success can leave us feeling unhappy, unsatisfied, and stuck.

Have you fallen into a creative rut? Do you feel "old" and out of touch in your job? Do others seem uncomfortable challenging your assumptions and ideas? Are market developments beginning to take you by surprise? These are just a few of the warning signs that you've fallen into the expertise trap. (For others, see the sidebar "Seven Warning Signs That You've Fallen into the Expertise Trap.") The solution is clear: Rededicate yourself to learning and growth. Turn back the clock and rediscover just a bit of what the Buddhists call *beginner's mind.*

But how? Many executives I encounter tell me they don't want to be handcuffed by their own expertise, but in the endless stream of meetings, emails, deadlines, and goals, they can't seem to find the time to learn new skills and approaches. They might attend a training session or two, or try to read the latest business bestseller in their spare time, but they remain wedded to their expert mindset and the same old, familiar ideas.

A few extraordinary leaders, however—some of the busiest and most productive—have developed strategies for escaping or avoiding the expertise trap. We can learn from their example.

Challenge Your Own Expertise

Experts cling to their beliefs in large part because their egos are attached to being "smart" or "the best" in their area of focus. To break this pattern, untether yourself from that identity, cultivate more modesty, and remind yourself of your intellectual limitations.

Check your ego.

Do you sometimes overshadow others so that you can look good? Do you dictate solutions to team members rather than rely on their capabilities? Do you put pressure on yourself to always appear "right"? How much pride do you take in the companywide accolades, the conference invitations, the industry awards?

If you are excessively gratified by the status that comes with your hard-won knowledge, try grounding yourself a little. Michael Bloomberg famously eschewed a lavish private office at his media company for a small, unremarkable cubicle. IKEA founder Ingvar Kamprad likewise lived simply, traveling inexpensively and driving an old car. Ian Cook, formerly Colgate-Palmolive's CEO and now its executive chairman, made sure to visit the locker room at plants and facilities to

Seven Warning Signs That You've Fallen into the Expertise Trap

1. *You're unfamiliar with new technologies or approaches in your industry.*

2. *When someone asks why you or the company does things in a certain way, you think, "Well, that's how we've always done it."*

3. *When making decisions, you focus on how much risk your options pose rather than on the opportunities they represent.*

4. *You discover that colleagues are working together in ways you haven't—such as Slack, texts rather than email, and mobile rather than desktop.*

5. *You keep proposing the same old strategies and tactics to address new challenges.*

6. *You try to make old solutions ever more precise rather than pioneering entirely new ones.*

7. *Millennials leave your team faster than they do other teams in your company.*

---

find out what was really going on. Some executives I've worked with also forgo their reserved parking spots and park in the back lot so that they can ride the shuttle with rank-and-file employees. They spotlight others' accomplishments at meetings and industry events and resist the urge to take credit for every success. They also spend time listening to team members instead of telling them what to do.

Methodically revisit your assumptions.
General Broderick made a number of ill-advised assumptions in his initial response to Katrina. You can avoid similar errors by regularly surfacing and testing your ingrained ideas. At the start of a new project or assignment, jot down three or more "theories" that underpin it. For instance, if your goal is to spur revenue growth by entering a new geographic market, you may be assuming that the market in question is attractive, that your products or services are appropriate for it, that you understand it as well as you do others, and so on. Analyze these assumptions one by one; decide which are valid and which you should discard; and change your strategy or approach accordingly.

One executive I coached, a senior leader in a midsize medical device company, was struggling to build market share, even though her company possessed great technology. When I asked her to do this exercise, she responded, "Medical specialists are the key gate-keepers. Our largest competitors have locked up relationships with the largest hospital systems. Our technology is the best on the market." When she analyzed those statements, she realized that although the specialists were gatekeepers, the more entrepreneurial among them might be open to working with new partners. And her company could support doctors who sought to break away from the big hospital systems and form their own, independent clinics. This thinking allowed her to bust out of the expertise trap and lead her company to compete in a nontraditional way, with excellent results.

Seek Out Fresh Ideas

Learning requires exposure to novelty. But when you're an expert, it's easy to become intellectually cloistered. Others don't or can't challenge you as often as they used to, and your authority or status can insulate you from pressure to learn and grow. Practiced regularly, the following exercises will introduce you to more diverse perspectives without detracting from other priorities.

Look to teammates as teachers.
Set aside a few minutes every month to reflect on the most important lessons or insights you gleaned from your team members, especially those whose expertise is less than or different from yours. Ask them open-ended questions to trigger their thoughts and encourage them to challenge your thinking and give you feedback. Then make certain that you take their comments seriously. Reward, rather than dismiss or criticize, those who speak up. Aron Ain, the CEO of the software company Kronos, has described his habit of walking around the office to kibitz or hold impromptu focus groups with employees at all levels of his organization to get their opinions on pressing business issues and glean new insights.

Another tactic is to create opportunities for junior colleagues to present on topics or issues that they find important but that you and other senior leaders aren't currently considering. These talks not only provide a great growth opportunity for younger people but also build your awareness of trends, technologies, or conditions relevant to your market. Kevin Cox took this approach in 2016, when he was the chief human resources officer at American Express: He asked some of the company's young high performers to participate in a special three-day ideation session and then present their best proposals for the business to senior leaders. But such events need not be so structured. The hedge fund legend Julian Robertson was known for holding informal sessions in which his junior analysts had a chance to argue for their ideas in front of their peers. Although he regularly pushed back, everyone understood and appreciated the spirit of lively debate he was trying to inculcate.

Tap new sources of talent.
Experts become creatively stuck and unable to learn because they surround themselves with people who look and sound just like them. The solution, of course, is to hire people with different functional, industry, or cultural backgrounds. Bill Walsh, the legendary San Francisco 49ers head coach, is venerated in the National Football League for hiring African-American assistant coaches and for creating an internship program that allowed the league to benefit from this formerly untapped talent pool. When Boston-based Eastern Bank set up an innovation lab in 2014, it brought in a category of worker previously unseen in its peer group of financial institutions: young creative types in jeans and flip-flops.

Think about your own team, company, and industry. Are any forms of diversity—ethnic, experiential, or other—unrepresented? What unique ideas or perspectives might your workplace gain from people with the missing background? Try recruiting some of them through atypical channels and then onboarding them with a light touch to retain their originality and curiosity. If you're not in a position to hire, seek out new voices at conferences or in your community, engage them in conversation, and bring them into your circle.

Add a role model or a learning buddy.
Marcus Samuelsson, the Ethiopian-Swedish executive chef at New York's acclaimed Red Rooster, looks to peers young and old for the inspiration to keep learning. One of them, Samuelsson says, is Leah Chase, a New Orleans chef in her nineties, who's "still questioning things with this same sense of excitement." Whom can you look to in the same way? Is anyone at your company or in your industry unusually dedicated to creativity and growth? Look up that person, follow her activities, and ask if you can check in regularly to compare ideas. What is she thinking about or reading? What does she do to broaden her horizons and stay current?

You can also cultivate "learning buddies"—colleagues who challenge your thinking and with whom you bounce around new ideas. The CEO of Scripps Health, Chris Van Gorder, consults with a group of "loyal friends" inside and outside the organization who he knows will provide "honest and sometimes tough feedback about my performance." The next time you're at an executive development program with participants from other businesses, make it a priority to connect with one or two people who might act as sounding boards for you.

Embrace Experimentalism

Leaders and managers stuck in the expertise trap don't just blind themselves to new ideas—they stop experimenting and taking risks, which ultimately leads to their downfall, because they're seldom learning anything new. It's important to push the limits of your comfort zone, even if there's a danger you'll fall on your face.

Pose frequent creative challenges for yourself.
Don't wait for others to spur you to experiment. Challenge yourself to break new ground by welcoming any unfamiliar or unusual assignments you get and treating them as "science experiments." Give yourself permission to set aside established rules and try different ways of accomplishing tasks. Doing things differently may not necessarily take longer (and may even lead to new efficiencies), but

it's still worth asking your boss for leeway, pointing out that you're actively experimenting and taking some risks for the team's benefit. Resist the urge to say no to novelty.

Challenging yourself with new pursuits outside work helps as well. Many successful leaders maintain creative hobbies as a way of staying fresh and "young" and bringing that mindset back to the office. Mark Zuckerberg reportedly taught himself a new language—Mandarin Chinese. David Solomon, the CEO of Goldman Sachs, makes a hobby of deejaying at Manhattan nightspots. The former Microsoft executive Nathan Myhrvold writes cookbooks.

Learn from mistakes.
Many expert managers downplay or ignore their own slipups, perhaps to protect their elevated view of their own capabilities. The outstanding leaders I've studied know that mistakes are to be acknowledged, not swept under the rug—especially when they themselves make them. How self-aware are you in this respect? Set aside time each month to think about the errors you made, big and small. Do you notice any patterns? Were you misaligned with your team? Did you rush to judgment when making a decision? Did any mistakes result from experiments you were trying? If so, what lessons can you capture? And what new experiments might you try to improve your performance?

Don't be afraid to go public with the fruits of this exercise. Hold quarterly "mistake" meetings at which you describe the biggest error you made in recent months and what you learned. Then invite team members to do the same. The Indian industrial magnate Ratan Tata has tried to institutionalize this practice by presiding over an annual award called Dare to Try, which recognizes employees for pursuing worthy but unsuccessful projects.

Exceptional leaders know that learning isn't ever "finished"—it must be a lifelong pursuit, as humbling as it is joyful. Their greatest fear isn't that their expertise and authority will be challenged but, rather, that they'll become complacent. Happily, we all have the power to meld learning into the very substance of our work.

Prevalent and dangerous as the expertise trap is, we can escape it—or avoid it entirely—by rebalancing our professional identities, checking our assumptions, listening to teammates, engaging different voices, finding new role models, challenging ourselves with new pursuits, and learning from our mistakes. We can cultivate a beginner's mind to go along with our expert perspective, pushing ourselves to new levels of creativity and performance.

Originally published March 2019. Reprint R1903L

Mindfulness in the Age of Complexity

by Ellen Langer and Alison Beard

OVER NEARLY FOUR DECADES, Ellen Langer's research on mindfulness has greatly influenced thinking across a range of fields, from behavioral economics to positive psychology. It reveals that by paying attention to what's going on around us, instead of operating on autopilot, we can reduce stress, unlock creativity, and boost performance. Her "counterclockwise" experiments, for example, demonstrated that elderly men could improve their health by simply acting as if it were 20 years earlier. In this interview with senior editor Alison Beard, Langer applies her thinking to leadership and management in an age of increasing chaos.

Let's start with the basics. What, exactly, is mindfulness? How do you define it?

Langer: Mindfulness is the process of actively noticing new things. When you do that, it puts you in the present. It makes you more sensitive to context and perspective. It's the essence of engagement. And it's energy-begetting, not energy-consuming. The mistake most people make is to assume it's stressful and exhausting—all this thinking. But what's stressful is all the mindless negative evaluations we make and the worry that we'll find problems and not be able to solve them.

We all seek stability. We want to hold things still, thinking that if we do, we can control them. But since everything is always changing, that doesn't work. Actually, it causes you to lose control.

Take work processes. When people say, "This is the way to do it," that's not true. There are always many ways, and the way you choose should depend on the current context. You can't solve today's problems with yesterday's solutions. So when someone says, "Learn this so it's second nature," let a bell go off in your head, because that means mindlessness. The rules you were given were the rules that worked for the person who created them, and the more different you are from that person, the worse they're going to work for you. When you're mindful, rules, routines, and goals guide you; they don't govern you.

What are some of the specific benefits of being more mindful, according to your research?

Better performance, for one. We did a study with symphony musicians, who, it turns out, are bored to death. They're playing the same pieces over and over again, and yet it's a high-status job that they can't easily walk away from. So we had groups of them perform. Some were told to replicate a previous performance they'd liked—that is, to play pretty mindlessly. Others were told to make their individual performance new in subtle ways—to play mindfully.

Remember: This wasn't jazz, so the changes were very subtle indeed. But when we played recordings of the symphonies for people who knew nothing about the study, they overwhelmingly preferred the mindfully played pieces. So here we had a group performance where everybody was doing their own thing, and it was better. There's this view that if you let everyone do their own thing, chaos will reign. When people are doing their own thing in a rebellious way, yes, it might. But if everyone is working in the same context and is fully present, there's no reason why you shouldn't get a superior coordinated performance.

There are many other advantages to mindfulness. It's easier to pay attention. You remember more of what you've done. You're more creative. You're able to take advantage of opportunities when they present themselves. You avert the danger not yet arisen. You like people better, and people like you better, because you're less evaluative. You're more charismatic.

The idea of procrastination and regret can go away, because if you know why you're doing something, you don't take yourself to task for not doing something else. If you're fully present when you decide to prioritize this task or work at this firm or create this product or pursue this strategy, why would you regret it?

I've been studying this for nearly 40 years, and for almost any measure, we find that mindfulness generates a more positive result. That makes sense when you realize it's a superordinate variable. No matter what you're doing—eating a sandwich, doing an interview, working on some gizmo, writing a report—you're doing it mindfully or mindlessly. When it's the former, it leaves an imprint on what you do. At the very highest levels of any field—*Fortune* 50 CEOs, the most impressive artists and musicians, the top athletes, the best teachers and mechanics—you'll find mindful people, because that's the only way to get there.

How have you shown a link between mindfulness and innovation?

With Gabriel Hammond, a graduate student, I ran a study where we asked participants to come up with new uses for products that had failed. We primed one group for mindlessness by telling them how the product had fallen short of its original intended use—to cite a famous example from 3M, a failed glue. We primed the other for mindfulness by simply describing the product's properties—a substance that adheres for only a short amount of time. Of course, the most creative ideas for new uses came from the second group.

I'm an artist as well as a researcher, writer, and consultant—each activity informs the others for me—and I got the idea to study mindfulness and mistakes when I was painting. I looked up and saw I was using ocher when I'd meant to use magenta, so I started trying to fix it. But then I realized I'd made the decision to use magenta only seconds before. People do this all the time. You start with uncertainty, you make a decision, and if you make a mistake, it's a calamity. But the path you were following was just a decision. You can change it at any time, and maybe an alternative will turn out better. When you're mindful, mistakes become friends.

How does being mindful make someone more charismatic?

We've shown this in a few studies. An early one was with magazine salespeople: The mindful ones sold more and were rated as more likable by buyers. More recently, we've looked at the bind that women executives face: If they act in strong, stereotypically masculine ways, they're seen as bitchy, but if they act feminine, they're seen as weak and not leadership material. So we asked two groups of women to give persuasive speeches. One group was told to act masculine, the other to act feminine. Then half of each group was instructed to give their speech mindfully, and we found that audiences preferred the mindful speakers, regardless of what gender role they were playing out.

And mindfulness also makes you less judgmental about others?

Yes. We all have a tendency to mindlessly pigeonhole people: He's rigid. She's impulsive. But when you freeze someone in that way, you don't get the chance to enjoy a relationship with them or use their talents. Mindfulness helps you to appreciate why people behave the way they do. It makes sense to them at the time, or else they wouldn't do it.

We did a study in which we asked people to rate their own character traits—the things they would most like to change and the things they most valued about themselves—and we found a big irony. The traits that people valued tended to be positive versions of the ones they wanted to change. So the reason I personally can't stop being impulsive is that I value being spontaneous. That means if you want to change my behavior, you'll have to persuade me not to like spontaneity. But chances are that when you see me from this proper perspective—spontaneous rather than impulsive—you won't want to change me.

Mindful Management

What else can managers do to be more mindful?

One tactic is to imagine that your thoughts are totally transparent. If they were, you wouldn't think awful things about other people. You'd find a way to understand their perspective.

And when you're upset about something—maybe someone turned in an assignment late, or didn't do it the way you wanted—ask yourself, "Is it a tragedy or an inconvenience?" It's probably the latter. Most of the things that get us upset are.

I also tell people to think about work/life *integration,* not balance. "Balance" suggests that the two are opposite and have nothing in common. But that's not true. They're both mostly about people. There are stresses in both. There are schedules to be met. If you keep them separate, you don't learn to transfer what you do successfully in one domain to the other. When we're mindful, we realize that categories are person-constructed and don't limit us.

Remember, too, that stress is not a function of events; it's a function of the view you take of events. You think a particular thing is going to happen and that when it does, it's going to be awful. But prediction is an illusion. We can't know what's going to happen. So give yourself five reasons you won't lose the job. Then think of five reasons why, if you did, it would be an advantage—new opportunities, more time with family, et cetera. Now you've gone from thinking it's definitely going to happen to thinking maybe it will and even if it does, you'll be OK.

If you feel overwhelmed by your responsibilities, use the same approach. Question the belief that you're the only one who can do it, that there's only one way to do it, and that the company will collapse if you don't do it. When you open your views to be mindful, the stress just dissipates.

Mindfulness helps you realize that there are no positive or negative outcomes. There's A, B, C, D, and more, each with its challenges and opportunities.

Give me some scenarios, and I'll explain how mindfulness helps.

I'm the leader of a team in dissent. People are arguing vehemently for different strategies, and I have to decide on one.

There's an old story about two people coming before a judge. One guy tells his side of the story, and the judge says, "That's right." The other guy tells his side of the story, and the judge says, "That's right." They say, "We can't both be right." And the judge says, "That's right." We have this mindless notion to settle disputes with a choice between this way or that way, or a compromise. But win-win solutions can almost always be sought. Instead of letting people lock into their positions, go back and open it up. Have opponents play the debate from the other side so that they realize there are good arguments either way. Then find a way for both of them to be right.

I'm an executive with lots of commitments who's facing a personal crisis.

If I couldn't do this interview because I was having a problem at home, I would say, "Alison, I hope you'll forgive me, but my mind is elsewhere right now because I'm having this crisis." And you might say, "Oh, no, I had a crisis last week. It's OK. I understand." And then, when the crisis was over, we could come back to what we were doing, but with a whole new relationship, which would set us up for all sorts of good things in the future.

I'm a boss giving a review to an underperforming employee.

Make clear that the evaluation is *your* perspective, not a universal one, which opens up the dialogue. Let's say a student or a worker adds one and one and gets one. The teacher or employer can just say "Wrong," or he can try to figure out how the person got to one. Then the worker says, "If you add one wad of chewing gum to another wad, one plus one equals one." Now the boss has learned something.

As a leader, you can walk around as if you're God and get everybody to quiver. But then you're not going to learn anything, because they're not going to tell you, and you're going to be lonely and unhappy. It doesn't have to be lonely at the top. You can be there and be open.

How do you create a more mindful organization?

When I'm doing consulting work with companies, I usually start by showing everyone how mindless they are, and what they're missing as a result. You can be mindless only if two conditions are met: You found the very best way of doing things, and nothing changes. Of course, those conditions can't be met. So if you're going to work, you should be there and notice things. Then I explain that there are alternative ways of getting anywhere, and in fact, you can't even be sure that the destination you've chosen is ultimately where you'll want to be. Everything looks different from different perspectives.

I tell leaders they should make not knowing OK—I don't know, you don't know, nobody knows—rather than acting like they know, so everyone else pretends *they* know, which leads to all sorts of discomfort and anxiety. Eliminate zero-accident policies. If you have a zero-accident policy, you're going to have a maximum-lying policy. Get people to ask, "Why? What are the benefits of doing it this way versus another way?" When you do that, everyone relaxes a little, and you're all better able to see and take advantage of opportunities.

I was working with a nursing home years ago, and a nurse walked in, complaining that one of the residents didn't want to go to the dining room. She wanted to stay in her room and eat peanut butter. So I butted in and said, "What's wrong with that?" Her answer was "What if everybody wants to do it?" And I said, "Well, if everybody did it, you'd save a lot of money on food. But, more seriously, it would tell you something about how the food is being prepared or served. If it's only one person occasionally, what's the big deal? If it happens all the time, there's an opportunity here."

I imagine you don't like checklists?

The first time you go through a checklist, it's fine. But after that, most people tend to do it mindlessly. So in aviation you have flaps up, throttle open, anti-ice off. But if snow is coming and the anti-ice is off, the plane crashes.

Checklists aren't bad if they require qualitative information to be obtained in that moment. For example, "Please note the weather conditions. Based on these conditions, should the anti-ice be on or off?" or "How is the patient's skin color different from yesterday?" If you ask questions that encourage mindfulness, you bring people into the present and you're more likely to avoid an accident.

Mindful, qualitative comments help in interpersonal relationships, too, by the way. If you're giving a compliment, "You look great" is not nearly as effective as something like "Your eyes are sparkling today." To say that, you have to be there, and people will recognize and appreciate it.

Mindfulness and Focus

The business environment has changed a lot since you began studying mindfulness. It's more complex and uncertain. We have new data and analysis coming at us all the time. So mindfulness becomes more important for navigating the chaos—but the chaos makes it a lot harder to be mindful.

I think chaos is a perception. People say that there's too much information, and I would say that there's no more information now than there was before. The difference is that people believe they have to know it—that the more information they have, the better the product is going to be and the more money the company is going to make. I don't think it depends as much on the amount of information someone has as on the way it's taken in. And that needs to be mindfully.

How has technology changed our ability to be mindful? Is it a help or a hindrance?

Again, one can bring mindfulness to anything. We've studied multitasking and found that if you're open and keep the boundaries loose, it can be an advantage. The information from one thing can help you with another. I think what we should do is learn from the way technology is fun and compelling and build that into our work.

HBR recently published an article on the importance of focus in which the author, Daniel Goleman, talks about the need for both exploration and exploitation. How do you balance mindfulness—constantly looking for the new—with the ability to buckle down and get things done?

Vigilance, or very focused attention, is probably mindless. If I'm racing through the woods on horseback, watching the branches so that I don't get hit in the face, I might miss the boulder on the ground, so then my horse stumbles and I'm thrown off. But I don't think that's what Dan means by focus. What you want is a soft openness—to be attentive to the things you're doing but not single-minded, because then you're missing other opportunities.

We hear the management community talking more about mindful-ness now. When did you realize that the ideas you've been studying for decades had become mainstream?

I was at a party, and two different people came up to me and said, "Your mindfulness is everywhere." Of course, I just saw a new film that starts with someone going around Harvard Square asking people what mindfulness is, and nobody knows. So there's still a lot of work to do.

What are you working on next?

The Langer Mindfulness Institute works in three arenas: health, aging, and the workplace. In health we want to see just how far we can push the mind-body notion. Years ago we did studies on chambermaids (who lost weight after being told their work was exercise) and vision (where people did better on eye tests that had them work up from large letters at the bottom to small ones at the top, creating the expectation that they would be able to read them). Now we're trying a mindfulness cure on many diseases that people think are uncontrollable to see if we can at least ameliorate the symptoms. We're also doing counterclockwise retreats around the world, start-ing in San Miguel de Allende, Mexico, using research-proven tech-niques to help people live boldly. And we're doing conferences and consulting on work/life integration, mindful leadership and strategy processes, stress reduction, and innovation, with companies such as Thorlo and Santander and NGOs such as CARE and Vermont's Energy Action Network.

I'm told that I drive my students crazy because I'm always coming up with new ideas. I'm thinking about maybe a mindfulness camp for children. One exercise might be to take a group of 20 kids and keep dividing them into subsets—male/female, younger/ older, dark hair/light hair, wearing black/not wearing black—until they realize that everyone is unique. As I've said for 30 years, the best way to decrease prejudice is to increase discrimination. We would also play games and midway through mix up the teams. Or maybe we'd give each child a chance to rewrite the rules of the game, so it becomes clear that performance is only a reflection of one's ability under certain circumstances. You know, if they allowed three serves in tennis, I would be a much better player.

What's the one thing about mindfulness you'd like every executive to remember?

It's going to sound corny, but I believe it fully: Life consists only of moments, nothing more than that. So if you make the moment matter, it all matters. You can be mindful, you can be mindless. You can win, you can lose. The worst case is to be mindless and lose. So when you're doing anything, be mindful, notice new things, make it meaningful to you, and you'll prosper.

Originally published March 2014. Reprint R1403D

Primal Leadership

The Hidden Driver of Great Performance.
by Daniel Goleman, Richard Boyatzis,
and Annie McKee

WHEN THE THEORY OF EMOTIONAL intelligence at work began to receive widespread attention, we frequently heard executives say—in the same breath, mind you—"That's incredible," and, "Well, I've known that all along." They were responding to our research that showed an incontrovertible link between an executive's emotional maturity, exemplified by such capabilities as self-awareness and empathy, and his or her financial performance. Simply put, the research showed that "good guys"—that is, emotionally intelligent men and women—finish first.

We've recently compiled two years of new research that, we suspect, will elicit the same kind of reaction. People will first exclaim, "No way," then quickly add, "But of course." We found that of all the elements affecting bottom-line performance, the importance of the leader's mood and its attendant behaviors are most surprising. That powerful pair set off a chain reaction: The leader's mood and behaviors drive the moods and behaviors of everyone else. A cranky and ruthless boss creates a toxic organization filled with negative underachievers who ignore opportunities; an inspirational, inclusive leader spawns acolytes for whom any challenge is surmountable. The final link in the chain is performance: profit or loss.

Our observation about the overwhelming impact of the leader's "emotional style," as we call it, is not a wholesale departure from our research into emotional intelligence. It does, however, represent a deeper analysis of our earlier assertion that a leader's emotional intelligence creates a certain culture or work environment. High levels of emotional intelligence, our research showed, create climates in which information sharing, trust, healthy risk-taking, and learning flourish. Low levels of emotional intelligence create climates rife with fear and anxiety. Because tense or terrified employees can be very productive in the short term, their organizations may post good results, but they never last.

Our investigation was designed in part to look at how emotional intelligence drives performance—in particular, at how it travels from the leader through the organization to bottom-line results. "What mechanism," we asked, "binds the chain together?" To answer that question, we turned to the latest neurological and psychological research. We also drew on our work with business leaders, observations by our colleagues of hundreds of leaders, and Hay Group data on the leadership styles of thousands of executives. From this body of research, we discovered that emotional intelligence is carried through an organization like electricity through wires. To be more specific, the leader's mood is quite literally contagious, spreading quickly and inexorably throughout the business.

We'll discuss the science of mood contagion in more depth later, but first let's turn to the key implications of our finding. If a leader's mood and accompanying behaviors are indeed such potent drivers of business success, then a leader's premier task—we would even say his primal task—is emotional leadership. A leader needs to make sure that not only is he regularly in an optimistic, authentic, high-energy mood, but also that, through his chosen actions, his followers feel and act that way, too. Managing for financial results, then, begins with the leader managing his inner life so that the right emotional and behavioral chain reaction occurs.

Managing one's inner life is not easy, of course. For many of us, it's our most difficult challenge. And accurately gauging how one's emotions affect others can be just as difficult. We know of one CEO, for example, who was certain that everyone saw him as upbeat and reliable; his direct reports told us they found his cheerfulness strained, even fake, and his decisions erratic. (We call this common

Idea in Brief

What *most* influences your company's bottom-line performance? The answer will surprise you—*and* make perfect sense: It's a leader's own mood.

Executives' emotional intelligence—their self-awareness, empathy, rapport with others—has clear links to their own performance. But new research shows that a leader's emotional style also drives everyone *else*'s moods and behaviors—through a neurological process called **mood contagion**. It's akin to "Smile and the whole world smiles with you."

Emotional intelligence travels through an organization like electricity over telephone wires. Depressed, ruthless bosses create toxic organizations filled with negative underachievers. But if you're an upbeat, inspirational leader, you cultivate positive employees who embrace and surmount even the toughest challenges.

Emotional leadership isn't just putting on a game face every day. It means understanding your impact on others—then adjusting your style accordingly. A difficult process of self-discovery—but essential *before* you can tackle your leadership responsibilities.

disconnect "CEO disease.") The implication is that primal leadership demands more than putting on a game face every day. It requires an executive to determine, through reflective analysis, how his emotional leadership drives the moods and actions of the organization, and then, with equal discipline, to adjust his behavior accordingly.

That's not to say that leaders can't have a bad day or week: Life happens. And our research doesn't suggest that good moods have to be high-pitched or nonstop—optimistic, sincere, and realistic will do. But there is no escaping the conclusion that a leader must first attend to the impact of his mood and behaviors before moving on to his wide panoply of other critical responsibilities. In this article, we introduce a process that executives can follow to assess how others experience their leadership, and we discuss ways to calibrate that impact. But first, we'll look at why moods aren't often discussed in the workplace, how the brain works to make moods contagious, and what you need to know about CEO disease.

Idea in Practice

Strengthening Your Emotional Leadership

Since few people have the guts to tell you the truth about your emotional impact, you must discover it on your own. The following process can help. It's based on brain science, as well as years of field research with executives. Use these steps to rewire your brain for greater emotional intelligence.

1. **Who do you want to be?** Imagine yourself as a highly effective leader. What do you see?

   Example: Sofia, a senior manager, often micromanaged others to ensure work was done "right." So she *imagined* herself in the future as an effective leader of her own company, enjoying trusting relationships with coworkers. She saw herself as relaxed, happy, and empowering. The exercise revealed gaps in her current emotional style.

2. **Who are you now?** To see your leadership style as others do, gather 360-degree feedback, especially from peers and subordinates. Identify your weaknesses *and* strengths.

3. **How do you get from here to there?** Devise a plan for closing the gap between who you are and who you want to be.

   Example: Juan, a marketing executive, was intimidating,

No Way! Yes Way

When we said earlier that people will likely respond to our new finding by saying "No way," we weren't joking. The fact is, the emotional impact of a leader is almost never discussed in the workplace, let alone in the literature on leadership and performance. For most people, "mood" feels too personal. Even though Americans can be shockingly candid about personal matters—witness the *Jerry Springer Show* and its ilk—we are also the most legally bound. We can't even ask the age of a job applicant. Thus, a conversation about an executive's mood or the moods he creates in his employees might be construed as an invasion of privacy.

We also might avoid talking about a leader's emotional style and its impact because, frankly, the topic feels soft. When was the last time you evaluated a subordinate's mood as part of her performance

impossible to please—a grouch. Charged with growing his company, he *needed* to be encouraging, optimistic—a coach with a vision. Setting out to understand others, he coached soccer, volunteered at a crisis center, and got to know subordinates by meeting outside of work. These new situations stimulated him to break old habits and try new responses.

4. **How do you make change stick?** Repeatedly rehearse new behaviors—physically *and* mentally—until they're automatic.

   Example: Tom, an executive, wanted to learn how to coach

rather than castigate struggling employees. Using his commuting time to visualize a difficult meeting with one employee, he envisioned asking questions and listening, and mentally rehearsed how he'd handle feeling impatient. This exercise prepared him to adopt new behaviors at the actual meeting.

5. **Who can help you?** Don't try to build your emotional skills alone—identify others who can help you navigate this difficult process. Managers at Unilever formed learning groups that helped them strengthen their leadership abilities by exchanging frank feedback and developing strong mutual trust.

appraisal? You may have alluded to it—"Your work is hindered by an often negative perspective," or "Your enthusiasm is terrific"—but it is unlikely you mentioned mood outright, let alone discussed its impact on the organization's results.

And yet our research undoubtedly will elicit a "But of course" reaction, too. Everyone knows how much a leader's emotional state drives performance because everyone has had, at one time or another, the inspirational experience of working for an upbeat manager or the crushing experience of toiling for a sour-spirited boss. The former made everything feel possible, and as a result, stretch goals were achieved, competitors beaten, and new customers won. The latter made work grueling. In the shadow of the boss's dark mood, other parts of the organization became "the enemy," colleagues became suspicious of one another, and customers slipped away.

Our research, and research by other social scientists, confirms the verity of these experiences. (There are, of course, rare cases when a brutal boss produces terrific results. We explore that dynamic in the sidebar "Those Wicked Bosses Who Win.") The studies are too numerous to mention here but, in aggregate, they show that when the leader is in a happy mood, the people around him view everything in a more positive light. That, in turn, makes them optimistic about achieving their goals, enhances their creativity and the efficiency of their decision making, and predisposes them to be helpful. Research conducted by Alice Isen at Cornell in 1999, for example, found that an upbeat environment fosters mental efficiency, making people better at taking in and understanding information, at using decision rules in complex judgments, and at being flexible in their thinking. Other research directly links mood and financial performance. In 1986, for instance, Martin Seligman and Peter Schulman of the University of Pennsylvania demonstrated that insurance agents who had a "glass half-full" outlook were far more able than their more pessimistic peers to persist despite rejections, and thus, they closed more sales. (For more information on these studies and a list of our research base, visit www.eiconsortium.org.)

Many leaders whose emotional styles create a dysfunctional environment are eventually fired. (Of course, that's rarely the stated reason; poor results are.) But it doesn't have to end that way. Just as a bad mood can be turned around, so can the spread of toxic feelings from an emotionally inept leader. A look inside the brain explains both why and how.

The Science of Moods

A growing body of research on the human brain proves that, for better or worse, leaders' moods affect the emotions of the people around them. The reason for that lies in what scientists call the open-loop nature of the brain's limbic system, our emotional center. A closed-loop system is self-regulating, whereas an open-loop system depends on external sources to manage itself. In other words, we rely on connections with other people to determine our moods. The

Those Wicked Bosses Who Win

EVERYONE KNOWS OF a rude and coercive CEO who, by all appearances, epitomizes the antithesis of emotional intelligence yet seems to reap great business results. If a leader's mood matters so much, how can we explain those mean-spirited, successful SOBs?

First, let's take a closer look at them. Just because a particular executive is the most visible, he may not actually lead the company. A CEO who heads a conglomerate may have no followers to speak of; it's his division heads who actively lead people and affect profitability.

Second, sometimes an SOB leader has strengths that counterbalance his caustic behavior, but they don't attract as much attention in the business press. In his early days at GE, Jack Welch exhibited a strong hand at the helm as he undertook a radical company turnaround. At that time and in that situation, Welch's firm, top-down style was appropriate. What got less press was how Welch subsequently settled into a more emotionally intelligent leadership style, especially when he articulated a new vision for the company and mobilized people to follow it.

Those caveats aside, let's get back to those infamous corporate leaders who seem to have achieved sterling business results despite their brutish approaches to leadership. Skeptics cite Bill Gates, for example, as a leader who gets away with a harsh style that should theoretically damage his company.

But our leadership model, which shows the effectiveness of specific leadership styles in specific situations, puts Gates's supposedly negative behaviors in a different light. (Our model is explained in detail in the HBR article "Leadership That Gets Results," which appeared in the March–April 2000 issue.) Gates is the achievement-driven leader par excellence, in an organization that has cherry-picked highly talented and motivated people. His apparently harsh leadership style—baldly challenging employees to surpass their past performance—can be quite effective when employees are competent, motivated, and need little direction—all characteristics of Microsoft's engineers.

In short, it's all too easy for a skeptic to argue against the importance of leaders who manage their moods by citing a "rough and tough" leader who achieved good business results despite his bad behavior. We contend that there are, of course, exceptions to the rule, and that in some specific business cases, an SOB boss resonates just fine. But in general, leaders who are jerks must reform or else their moods and actions will eventually catch up with them.

open-loop limbic system was a winning design in evolution because it let people come to one another's emotional rescue—enabling a mother, for example, to soothe her crying infant.

The open-loop design serves the same purpose today as it did thousands of years ago. Research in intensive care units has shown, for example, that the comforting presence of another person not only lowers the patient's blood pressure but also slows the secretion of fatty acids that block arteries. Another study found that three or more incidents of intense stress within a year (for example, serious financial trouble, being fired, or a divorce) triples the death rate in socially isolated middle-aged men, but it has no impact on the death rate of men with many close relationships.

Scientists describe the open loop as "interpersonal limbic regulation"; one person transmits signals that can alter hormone levels, cardiovascular functions, sleep rhythms, even immune functions, inside the body of another. That's how couples are able to trigger surges of oxytocin in each other's brains, creating a pleasant, affectionate feeling. But in all aspects of social life, our physiologies intermingle. Our limbic system's open-loop design lets other people change our very physiology and hence, our emotions.

Even though the open loop is so much a part of our lives, we usually don't notice the process. Scientists have captured the attunement of emotions in the laboratory by measuring the physiology—such as heart rate—of two people sharing a good conversation. As the interaction begins, their bodies operate at different rhythms. But after 15 minutes, the physiological profiles of their bodies look remarkably similar.

Researchers have seen again and again how emotions spread irresistibly in this way whenever people are near one another. As far back as 1981, psychologists Howard Friedman and Ronald Riggio found that even completely nonverbal expressiveness can affect other people. For example, when three strangers sit facing one another in silence for a minute or two, the most emotionally expressive of the three transmits his or her mood to the other two—without a single word being spoken.

Smile and the World Smiles with You

REMEMBER THAT OLD cliché? It's not too far from the truth. As we've shown, mood contagion is a real neurological phenomenon, but not all emotions spread with the same ease. A 1999 study conducted by Sigal Barsade at the Yale School of Management showed that, among working groups, cheerfulness and warmth spread easily, while irritability caught on less so, and depression least of all.

It should come as no surprise that laughter is the most contagious of all emotions. Hearing laughter, we find it almost impossible not to laugh or smile, too. That's because some of our brain's open-loop circuits are designed to detect smiles and laughter, making us respond in kind. Scientists theorize that this dynamic was hardwired into our brains ages ago because smiles and laughter had a way of cementing alliances, thus helping the species survive.

The main implication here for leaders undertaking the primal task of managing their moods and the moods of others is this: Humor hastens the spread of an upbeat climate. But like the leader's mood in general, humor must resonate with the organization's culture and its reality. Smiles and laughter, we would posit, are only contagious when they're genuine.

The same holds true in the office, boardroom, or shop floor; group members inevitably "catch" feelings from one another. In 2000, Caroline Bartel at New York University and Richard Saavedra at the University of Michigan found that in 70 work teams across diverse industries, people in meetings together ended up sharing moods—both good and bad—within two hours. One study asked teams of nurses and accountants to monitor their moods over weeks; researchers discovered that their emotions tracked together, and they were largely independent of each team's shared hassles. Groups, therefore, like individuals, ride emotional roller coasters, sharing everything from jealousy to angst to euphoria. (A good mood, incidentally, spreads most swiftly by the judicious use of humor. For more on this, see the sidebar "Smile and the World Smiles with You.")

Moods that start at the top tend to move the fastest because everyone watches the boss. They take their emotional cues from him. Even when the boss isn't highly visible—for example, the CEO

Get Happy, Carefully

GOOD MOODS GALVANIZE good performance, but it doesn't make sense for a leader to be as chipper as a blue jay at dawn if sales are tanking or the business is going under. The most effective executives display moods and behaviors that match the situation at hand, with a healthy dose of optimism mixed in. They respect how other people are feeling—even if it is glum or defeated—but they also model what it looks like to move forward with hope and humor.

This kind of performance, which we call resonance, is for all intents and purposes the four components of emotional intelligence in action.

Self-awareness, perhaps the most essential of the emotional intelligence competencies, is the ability to read your own emotions. It allows people to know their strengths and limitations and feel confident about their self-worth. Resonant leaders use self-awareness to gauge their own moods accurately, and they intuitively know how they are affecting others.

Self-management is the ability to control your emotions and act with honesty and integrity in reliable and adaptable ways. Resonant leaders don't let their occasional bad moods seize the day; they use self-management to leave it outside the office or to explain its source to people in a reasonable manner, so they know where it's coming from and how long it might last.

Social awareness includes the key capabilities of empathy and organizational intuition. Socially aware executives do more than sense other people's emotions, they show that they care. Further, they are experts at reading the currents of office politics. Thus, resonant leaders often keenly understand how their words and actions make others feel, and they are sensitive enough to change them when that impact is negative.

Relationship management, the last of the emotional intelligence competencies, includes the abilities to communicate clearly and convincingly,

who works behind closed doors on an upper floor—his attitude affects the moods of his direct reports, and a domino effect ripples throughout the company.

Call That CEO a Doctor

If the leader's mood is so important, then he or she had better get into a good one, right? Yes, but the full answer is more complicated than that. A leader's mood has the greatest impact on performance

disarm conflicts, and build strong personal bonds. Resonant leaders use these skills to spread their enthusiasm and solve disagreements, often with humor and kindness.

As effective as resonant leadership is, it is just as rare. Most people suffer through dissonant leaders whose toxic moods and upsetting behaviors wreak havoc before a hopeful and realistic leader repairs the situation.

Consider what happened recently at an experimental division of the BBC, the British media giant. Even though the group's 200 or so journalists and editors had given their best effort, management decided to close the division.

The shutdown itself was bad enough, but the brusque, contentious mood and manner of the executive sent to deliver the news to the assembled staff incited something beyond the expected frustration. People became enraged—at both the decision and the bearer of the news. The executive's cranky mood and delivery created an atmosphere so threatening that he had to call security to be ushered from the room.

The next day, another executive visited the same staff. His mood was somber and respectful, as was his behavior. He spoke about the importance of journalism to the vibrancy of a society and of the calling that had drawn them all to the field in the first place. He reminded them that no one goes into journalism to get rich—as a profession its finances have always been marginal, job security ebbing and flowing with the larger economic tides. He recalled a time in his own career when he had been let go and how he had struggled to find a new position—but how he had stayed dedicated to the profession. Finally, he wished them well in getting on with their careers.

The reaction from what had been an angry mob the day before? When this resonant leader finished speaking, the staff cheered.

when it is upbeat. But it must also be in tune with those around him. We call this dynamic *resonance*. (For more on this, see the sidebar "Get Happy, Carefully.")

We found that an alarming number of leaders do not really know if they have resonance with their organizations. Rather, they suffer from CEO disease; its one unpleasant symptom is the sufferer's near-total ignorance about how his mood and actions appear to the organization. It's not that leaders don't care how they are perceived; most do. But they incorrectly assume that they can decipher this information themselves. Worse, they think that if they are having a negative effect, someone will tell them. They're wrong.

As one CEO in our research explains, "I so often feel I'm not getting the truth. I can never put my finger on it, because no one is actually lying to me. But I can sense that people are hiding information or camouflaging key facts. They aren't lying, but neither are they telling me everything I need to know. I'm always second-guessing."

People don't tell leaders the whole truth about their emotional impact for many reasons. Sometimes they are scared of being the bearer of bad news—and getting shot. Others feel it isn't their place to comment on such a personal topic. Still others don't realize that what they really want to talk about is the effects of the leader's emotional style—that feels too vague. Whatever the reason, the CEO can't rely on his followers to spontaneously give him the full picture.

Taking Stock

The process we recommend for self-discovery and personal reinvention is neither newfangled nor born of pop psychology, like so many self-help programs offered to executives today. Rather, it is based on three streams of research into how executives can improve the emotional intelligence capabilities most closely linked to effective leadership. (Information on these research streams can also be found at www.eiconsortium.org.). In 1989, one of us (Richard Boyatzis) began drawing on this body of research to design the five-step process itself, and since then, thousands of executives have used it successfully.

Unlike more traditional forms of coaching, our process is based on brain science. A person's emotional skills—the attitude and abilities with which someone approaches life and work—are not genetically hardwired, like eye color and skin tone. But in some ways they might as well be, because they are so deeply embedded in our neurology.

A person's emotional skills do, in fact, have a genetic component. Scientists have discovered, for instance, the gene for shyness—which is not a mood, per se, but it can certainly drive a person toward a persistently quiet demeanor, which may be read as a "down" mood.

Other people are preternaturally jolly—that is, their relentless cheerfulness seems preternatural until you meet their peppy parents. As one executive explains, "All I know is that ever since I was a baby, I have always been happy. It drives some people crazy, but I couldn't get blue if I tried. And my brother is the exact same way; he saw the bright side of life, even during his divorce."

Even though emotional skills are partly inborn, experience plays a major role in how the genes are expressed. A happy baby whose parents die or who endures physical abuse may grow into a melancholy adult. A cranky toddler may turn into a cheerful adult after discovering a fulfilling avocation. Still, research suggests that our range of emotional skills is relatively set by our mid-20s and that our accompanying behaviors are, by that time, deep-seated habits. And therein lies the rub: The more we act a certain way—be it happy, depressed, or cranky—the more the behavior becomes ingrained in our brain circuitry, and the more we will continue to feel and act that way.

That's why emotional intelligence matters so much for a leader. An emotionally intelligent leader can monitor his or her moods through self-awareness, change them for the better through self-management, understand their impact through empathy, and act in ways that boost others' moods through relationship management.

The following five-part process is designed to rewire the brain toward more emotionally intelligent behaviors. The process begins with imagining your ideal self and then coming to terms with your real self, as others experience you. The next step is creating a tactical plan to bridge the gap between ideal and real, and after that, to practice those activities. It concludes with creating a community of colleagues and family—call them change enforcers—to keep the process alive. Let's look at the steps in more detail.

"Who do I want to be?"

Sofia, a senior manager at a northern European telecommunications company, knew she needed to understand how her emotional leadership affected others. Whenever she felt stressed, she tended to communicate poorly and take over subordinates' work so that the job would be done "right." Attending leadership seminars hadn't changed her habits, and neither had reading management books or working with mentors.

When Sofia came to us, we asked her to imagine herself eight years from now as an effective leader and to write a description of a typical day. "What would she be doing?" we asked. "Where would she live? Who would be there? How would it feel?" We urged her to consider her deepest values and loftiest dreams and to explain how those ideals had become a part of her everyday life.

Sofia pictured herself leading her own tight-knit company staffed by ten colleagues. She was enjoying an open relationship with her daughter and had trusting relationships with her friends and coworkers. She saw herself as a relaxed and happy leader and parent, and as loving and empowering to all those around her.

In general, Sofia had a low level of self-awareness: She was rarely able to pinpoint why she was struggling at work and at home. All she could say was, "Nothing is working right." This exercise, which prompted her to picture what life would look like if everything were going right, opened her eyes to the missing elements in her emotional style. She was able to see the impact she had on people in her life.

"Who am I now?"

In the next step of the discovery process, you come to see your leadership style as others do. This is both difficult and dangerous. Difficult, because few people have the guts to tell the boss or a colleague what he's really like. And dangerous, because such information can sting or even paralyze. A small bit of ignorance about yourself isn't always a bad thing: Ego-defense mechanisms have their advantages. Research by Martin Seligman shows that high-functioning people generally feel more optimistic about their prospects and possibilities than average performers. Their rose-colored lenses, in fact, fuel the enthusiasm and energy that make the unexpected and the extraordinary achievable. Playwright Henrik Ibsen called such self-delusions "vital lies," soothing mistruths we let ourselves believe in order to face a daunting world.

But self-delusion should come in very small doses. Executives should relentlessly seek the truth about themselves, especially since it is sure to be somewhat diluted when they hear it anyway. One way to get the truth is to keep an extremely open attitude toward critiques. Another is to seek out negative feedback, even cultivating a colleague or two to play devil's advocate.

We also highly recommend gathering feedback from as many people as possible—including bosses, peers, and subordinates. Feedback from subordinates and peers is especially helpful because it most accurately predicts a leader's effectiveness, two, four, and even seven years out, according to research by Glenn McEvoy at Utah State and Richard Beatty at Rutgers University.

Of course, 360-degree feedback doesn't specifically ask people to evaluate your moods, actions, and their impact. But it does reveal how people experience you. For instance, when people rate how well you listen, they are really reporting how well they think you hear them. Similarly, when 360-degree feedback elicits ratings about coaching effectiveness, the answers show whether or not people feel you understand and care about them. When the feedback uncovers low scores on, say, openness to new ideas, it means that people experience you as inaccessible or unapproachable or both. In sum, all you need to know about your emotional impact is in 360-degree feedback, if you look for it.

One last note on this second step. It is, of course, crucial to identify your areas of weakness. But focusing only on your weaknesses can be dispiriting. That's why it is just as important, maybe even more so, to understand your strengths. Knowing where your real self overlaps with your ideal self will give you the positive energy you need to move forward to the next step in the process—bridging the gaps.

"How do I get from here to there?"

Once you know who you want to be and have compared it with how people see you, you need to devise an action plan. For Sofia, this meant planning for a real improvement in her level of self-awareness. So she asked each member of her team at work to give her feedback—weekly, anonymously, and in written form—about her mood and performance and their affect on people. She also committed herself to three tough but achievable tasks: spending an hour each day reflecting on her behavior in a journal, taking a class on group dynamics at a local college, and enlisting the help of a trusted colleague as an informal coach.

Consider, too, how Juan, a marketing executive for the Latin American division of a major integrated energy company, completed this step. Juan was charged with growing the company in his home country of Venezuela as well as in the entire region—a job that would require him to be a coach and a visionary and to have an encouraging, optimistic outlook. Yet 360-degree feedback revealed that Juan was seen as intimidating and internally focused. Many of his direct reports saw him as a grouch—impossible to please at his worst, and emotionally draining at his best.

Identifying this gap allowed Juan to craft a plan with manageable steps toward improvement. He knew he needed to hone his powers of empathy if he wanted to develop a coaching style, so he committed to various activities that would let him practice that skill. For instance, Juan decided to get to know each of his subordinates better; if he understood more about who they were, he thought, he'd be more able to help them reach their goals. He made plans with each employee to meet outside of work, where they might be more comfortable revealing their feelings.

Juan also looked for areas outside of his job to forge his missing links—for example, coaching his daughter's soccer team and volunteering at a local crisis center. Both activities helped him to experiment with how well he understood others and to try out new behaviors.

Again, let's look at the brain science at work. Juan was trying to overcome ingrained behaviors—his approach to work had taken hold over time, without his realizing it. Bringing them into awareness was a crucial step toward changing them. As he paid more attention, the situations that arose—while listening to a colleague, coaching soccer, or talking on the phone to someone who was distraught—all became cues that stimulated him to break old habits and try new responses.

Resonance in Times of Crisis

WHEN TALKING ABOUT LEADERS' moods, the importance of resonance cannot be overstated. While our research suggests that leaders should generally be upbeat, their behavior must be rooted in realism, especially when faced with a crisis.

Consider the response of Bob Mulholland, senior VP and head of the client relations group at Merrill Lynch, to the terrorist attacks in New York. On September 11, 2001, Mulholland and his staff in Two World Financial Center felt the building rock, then watched as smoke poured out of a gaping hole in the building directly across from theirs. People started panicking: Some ran frantically from window to window. Others were paralyzed with fear. Those with relatives working in the World Trade Center were terrified for their safety. Mulholland knew he had to act: "When there's a crisis, you've got to show people the way, step by step, and make sure you're taking care of their concerns."

He started by getting people the information they needed to "unfreeze." He found out, for instance, which floors employees' relatives worked on and assured them that they'd have enough time to escape. Then he calmed the panic-stricken, one at a time. "We're getting out of here now," he said quietly, "and you're coming with me. Not the elevator, take the stairs." He remained calm and decisive, yet he didn't minimize people's emotional responses. Thanks to him, everyone escaped before the towers collapsed.

Mulholland's leadership didn't end there. Recognizing that this event would touch each client personally, he and his team devised a way for financial consultants to connect with their clients on an emotional level. They called every client to ask, "How are you? Are your loved ones okay? How are you feeling?" As Mulholland explains, "There was no way to pick up and do business as usual. The first order of 'business' was letting our clients know we really do care."

Bob Mulholland courageously performed one of the most crucial emotional tasks of leadership: He helped himself and his people find meaning in the face of chaos and madness. To do so, he first attuned to and expressed the shared emotional reality. That's why the direction he eventually articulated resonated at the gut level. His words and his actions reflected what people were feeling in their hearts.

This cueing for habit change is neural as well as perceptual. Researchers at the University of Pittsburgh and Carnegie Mellon University have shown that as we mentally prepare for a task, we activate the prefrontal cortex—the part of the brain that moves us into action. The greater the prior activation, the better we do at the task.

Such mental preparation becomes particularly important when we're trying to replace an old habit with a better one. As neuroscientist Cameron Carter at the University of Pittsburgh found, the prefrontal cortex becomes particularly active when a person prepares to overcome a habitual response. The aroused prefrontal cortex marks the brain's focus on what's about to happen. Without that arousal, a person will reenact tried-and-true but undesirable routines: The executive who just doesn't listen will once again cut off his subordinate, a ruthless leader will launch into yet another critical attack, and so on. That's why a learning agenda is so important. Without one, we literally do not have the brainpower to change.

"How do I make change stick?"

In short, making change last requires practice. The reason, again, lies in the brain. It takes doing and redoing, over and over, to break old neural habits. A leader must rehearse a new behavior until it becomes automatic—that is, until he's mastered it at the level of implicit learning. Only then will the new wiring replace the old.

While it is best to practice new behaviors, as Juan did, sometimes just envisioning them will do. Take the case of Tom, an executive who wanted to close the gap between his real self (perceived by colleagues and subordinates to be cold and hard driving) and his ideal self (a visionary and a coach).

Tom's learning plan involved finding opportunities to step back and coach his employees rather than jumping down their throats when he sensed they were wrong. Tom also began to spend idle moments during his commute thinking through how to handle encounters he would have that day. One morning, while en route to a breakfast meeting with an employee who seemed to be bungling a project, Tom ran through a positive scenario in his mind. He asked questions and listened to be sure he fully understood the situation before trying to solve the problem. He anticipated feeling impatient, and he rehearsed how he would handle these feelings.

Studies on the brain affirm the benefits of Tom's visualization technique: Imagining something in vivid detail can fire the same brain cells actually involved in doing that activity. The new brain circuitry appears to go through its paces, strengthening connections, even when we merely repeat the sequence in our minds. So to alleviate the fears associated with trying out riskier ways of leading, we should first visualize some likely scenarios. Doing so will make us feel less awkward when we actually put the new skills into practice.

Experimenting with new behaviors and seizing opportunities inside and outside of work to practice them—as well as using such methods as mental rehearsal—eventually triggers in our brains the neural connections necessary for genuine change to occur. Even so, lasting change doesn't happen through experimentation and brainpower alone. We need, as the song goes, a little help from our friends.

"Who can help me?"

The fifth step in the self-discovery and reinvention process is creating a community of supporters. Take, for example, managers at Unilever who formed learning groups as part of their executive development process. At first, they gathered to discuss their careers and how to provide leadership. But because they were also charged with discussing their dreams and their learning goals, they soon realized that they were discussing both their work and their personal lives. They developed a strong mutual trust and began relying on one another for frank feedback as they worked on strengthening their leadership abilities. When this happens, the business benefits through stronger performance. Many professionals today have created similar groups, and for good reason. People we trust let us try out unfamiliar parts of our leadership repertoire without risk.

We cannot improve our emotional intelligence or change our leadership style without help from others. We not only practice with other people but also rely on them to create a safe environment in which to experiment. We need to get feedback about how our actions affect others and to assess our progress on our learning agenda.

In fact, perhaps paradoxically, in the self-directed learning process we draw on others every step of the way—from articulating and refining our ideal self and comparing it with the reality to the final assessment that affirms our progress. Our relationships offer us the very context in which we understand our progress and comprehend the usefulness of what we're learning.

Mood over Matter

When we say that managing your mood and the moods of your followers is the task of primal leadership, we certainly don't mean to suggest that mood is all that matters. As we've noted, your actions are critical, and mood and actions together must resonate with the organization and with reality. Similarly, we acknowledge all the other challenges leaders must conquer—from strategy to hiring to new product development. It's all in a long day's work.

But taken as a whole, the message sent by neurological, psychological, and organizational research is startling in its clarity. Emotional leadership is the spark that ignites a company's performance, creating a bonfire of success or a landscape of ashes. Moods matter that much.

Originally published in December 2001. Reprint Ro111C

The Right Way to Form New Habits

by James Clear and Alison Beard

*Editor's Note: The transcript of this audio interview (originally pub-
lished on December 31, 2019) has been lightly edited for clarity.*

We spoke with James Clear, entrepreneur and author of the book
Atomic Habits: An Easy and Proven Way to Build Good Habits and
Break Bad Ones, *about why success requires discipline. It's something
we've seen time and time again in the stories of great leaders. They
might get up at 4 a.m. every day, read a book a week, or have a tried-
and-true system for client outreach or interviewing.*

*Many of these people seem to have superhuman ambitions and
work ethics. But there's another way of looking at their achievements:
They've developed great habits. While most of us are slipping into
bad habits—doing the easiest work first, making impulsive decisions,
watching TV instead of studying a new idea, or even not getting enough
sleep—high achievers are sticking to a plan and getting more out of
their careers and lives as a result.*

*Whether your goal is to learn a new skill, finish a big project, or
attend more networking events, Clear says there are simple and easy
ways of developing better habits to help you get where you want
to go.*

*At the taping of this interview, we're about to start a new year, a new
decade even. For those of us who make New Year's resolutions and
then quickly fail at sticking to them, how can we do better?*

Clear: There are a lot of entry points to discussing habits through
resolutions. So, I'll give you two. The first idea is that a lot of the
time we start with goals or ambitions or resolutions that are really

big, and simply scaling your habits down—or scaling those behaviors down—to something that's simple and easy to do is certainly a way to be more effective in the New Year, to increase the likelihood that you stick with your goal.

I refer to this as "the two-minute rule." You basically take whatever habit you're trying to build and scale it down to something that takes two minutes or less to do. So, "Read 30 books next year" becomes "Read one page a day." Or "Do yoga four days a week" becomes "Take out my yoga mat."

And sometimes people resist that a little, because they think, "OK, I know the real goal isn't just to take my yoga mat out each day. I know I actually want to do the workout." However, I think this is a deep truth about habits and certainly applies to New Year's resolutions too: The habit must be established before it can be improved. It has to become the standard in your life before you can worry about optimizing or scaling it up from there.

And then the second thing is to focus more on your identity than on the outcome. A lot of the discussion on New Year's resolutions is about how many books we want to read, or how much weight we want to lose, or how much more money we'd like to earn next year, or whatever it is. But I think it's a useful question to ask yourself: "Who is the type of person that could achieve those outcomes?"

Who is the type of person who could lose 20 pounds, let's say? Well, maybe it's the type of person who doesn't miss workouts. And then your focus becomes building habits that reinforce that identity rather than achieving a particular outcome. And you can trust that the outcome will come naturally if you show up as a specific type of person each day.

It's funny you mention the identity piece of this. In the book, you write that we limit ourselves by saying things such as, "I'm not a morning person. I'm bad at remembering names. I'm always late. I'm not good with technology. I'm horrible at math."

And I almost laughed out loud when I read that because I say all of these things about myself even though I know that waking up earlier, remembering names, being on time, or getting better at math and

technology would make me much better at my job as a business jour-
nalist. So how do I change that mindset about myself?

I think that perhaps the real reason that habits matter is that they can shift your internal narrative. They can change your self-image. And the first time you do something, or the 10th time, or maybe even the 100th time, you may not think differently about yourself yet or have adopted a new identity fully.

But at some point, when you keep showing up, you cross this invisible threshold and you start to think, "Hey, maybe I am a studious person," or "Maybe I am a clean and organized person after all."

Every action you take is like a vote for the type of person you want to become. And so, the more you show up and perform habits, the more you cast votes for being a certain type of person, the more you build up this body of evidence—the likelier you are to realize that, "Hey, this is who I actually am."

And I think this is what makes my approach a little bit different than what you often hear about behavior change, which is something like, "Fake it till you make it." "Fake it till you make it" is asking you to believe something positive about yourself without having evidence for it. And we have a word for beliefs that don't have evidence: We call them delusions.

At some point your brain doesn't like this mismatch between what you keep saying you are and what your behavior is. Behavior and beliefs are a two-way street, and my argument is that you should let the behavior lead the way. Start with one push-up. Start with writing one sentence. Start with meditating for one minute. Whatever it is.

Because, at least in that moment, you cannot deny that you were a writer, or you were the type of person who doesn't miss workouts, or you were a meditator. And in the long run that's the real objective. The goal's not to run a marathon. The goal is to become a runner. And once you start assigning those new identities to yourself, you're not even really pursuing behavior change anymore. You're just acting in alignment with the type of person you see yourself being. And so I think, in that way, true behavior change is really identity change.

How can we bring this into a work context? How have you seen bad habits derail people and the development of good habits really propel them forward?

So, specifically with work, I think we can broadly lump habits into two categories. The first category is what you might call *habits of energy*. For example, building good sleep habits. That's sort of a meta-habit; if you get that dialed in, you're in a better position to perform almost any other habit. And if you're not well rested, then you're kind of hindering yourself in your performance each day.

Pretty much any health-related habit falls in that bucket. Exercise, stress reduction, good nutrition habits, they're all in that habits-of-energy bucket. But the second category, and the one that is maybe more directly related to knowledge work, is what I would call *habits of attention*.

For almost all of us—and certainly for people who spend their time doing knowledge work or who are paid for the value of their creativity—the ideas you come up with are often a product of where you allocate your attention. So, what you read and what you consume often are the precursors to the thoughts you have, or to the creative or innovative ideas you come up with.

By improving your consumption habits, or your attention habits, you can dramatically improve the output you have at work. And we all live in this world with a fire hose of information. And so the ability to curate, to edit, to refine, to filter your information feed—whether that be the people you follow on Twitter, the articles you read each day, the news sources you select, or the books you read—those are very important decisions that determine the downstream output. This is about what you're bringing in.

But there are also other habits you can build, the purpose of which is not to bring things in but to cut things out. It's to reduce the distractions. For example, one habit I've been following for the last year or so, which I probably do about 90% of days, is to leave my phone in another room until lunch each day.

I have a home office and if I bring my phone in with me and it's on the desk, I'm like everybody else: I'll check it every three minutes just because it's there. But if I leave it in another room, then it's only

30 seconds away, but I never go get it. And what's always so interesting to me is the question, Did I want it or not? In one sense, I did want it badly enough to check it every three minutes when it was next to me, but in another sense I never wanted it badly enough to walk the 30 seconds to go get it when I put it in another room.

And I think we see this so much with habits of technology and convenience and modern society—and particularly with smartphones or apps. Actions are so frictionless, so convenient, so simple, so easy that we find ourselves being pulled into them at the slightest whim. Just the faintest hint of desire is enough to pull us off course.

So if you can redesign your environment, whether it's your desk at work or your office at home or the kitchen counter, to make the actions of least resistance the good and productive ones, and increase the friction of the things that take your attention away, I think you will often find those habits of attention start to be allocated to more-productive areas. To recap, I would say that habits of energy and habits of attention are the two places to focus if you want to increase your work output.

What about habits of proactivity? Forcing yourself to do more sales calls or go to more networking events, that sort of thing?

Certainly being proactive is a really important part of life. I think it's a great quality to have. The language that you used about "forcing yourself" to do sales calls, or "forcing yourself" to go to networking events or whatever . . .

Motivating. Let's say "motivating."

Sure, OK. I do think that phrasing—"motivating"—is probably a better way to look at it. There are many ways to do this, or to accomplish the same outcome. And so, ask yourself questions like: What is the real goal here? What would this look like if it was easy? What is a way to achieve this that doesn't add friction to my life?

Those are important questions to ask and revisit, no matter what task you're trying to achieve. Because I think what most of us find, what is implicitly known, is that there are many behaviors that naturally pull us in, whether that's because they're attractive and convenient or because they just kind of naturally align with our personality or our strengths. There can be a variety of reasons. But focusing on those things that naturally pull you in, rather than things you have to push upon yourself, I think is generally the right approach to take.

As an example, you mentioned networking. Certainly having a strong network is a very powerful and important thing in the modern work environment. But for some people, if you feel more introverted, or you just don't gravitate toward chitchat or whatever, going to a networking event kind of sounds like a nightmare.

The good news is that we live in a time when there are actually many ways to network. The most effective networking strategy is to do great work and then share it publicly. And that could mean writing an interesting article; it could be recording a podcast or doing a YouTube video. Whatever it is, just do something interesting and then put that out into the world. It kind of becomes a magnet for people who are like-minded and interested in the same things. It becomes a much more powerful form of networking than going to a cocktail hour.

My point here is that by asking those questions (What is the real goal? What would this look like if it was easy? Is there a way to add this or do this or achieve this that would not bring friction into my life?), you often find that there are interesting alternative pathways for achieving a particular outcome.

Speaking of buckling down to write something or working on your most important project, what are some ways that you can encourage yourself to do that work first, to spend the most time on it?

There is a story in *Atomic Habits* about Twyla Tharp, a famous dance choreographer and instructor. She's a huge fan of habits and has had all these great routines throughout her career. For instance, she has this exercise routine that she does each morning, where she works out for two hours at the gym. But she always says the habit is not the training in the gym. The habit is hailing the cab outside her apartment.

And I think that's actually very instructive for anybody who's looking to do this kind of important work that you mention. How can I focus on the area of highest importance or the highest use of my time? And the answer is to make the habit the entry point, not the end point. View your habits as an entrance ramp to a highway.

What are the productive things that I should be spending time on? What are the highest-value tasks? Walk back the behavioral chain and try to find the tip of the spear. What is that entry point? And then if you can figure out what that first minute or two minutes look like, if you can automate that—the hailing of the cab for instance— then you find that the next chunk of time kind of falls into place automatically.

You write about how Victor Hugo developed a novel way of encouraging himself to sit down and work.

Hugo, a famous author, wrote a variety of books, and the story goes that when he signed the deal to write *The Hunchback of Notre Dame,* he got his advance and signed the contract and then did what a lot of us would do: He spent the next year procrastinating. He had friends over for dinner. He traveled. He went out to eat. He basically did everything except work on the book.

And this was before technology was there to distract him.

Right. I think maybe we just gravitate toward more fun and satisfying and entertaining uses of time, regardless of the time period.

Eventually, his publisher got wind of this and told him, "Dude, something has to change. Either you finish the book in six months or we're going to ask for the money back." Now he's facing this ultimatum, so Hugo brought his assistant into his chambers and they gathered up all his clothes and put them in this large chest, locked it up, and took it out of the house. And so all he was left with was this large shawl, this robe.

And suddenly, he had no clothes that were suitable for entertaining guests. No clothes that were suitable for traveling. No clothes that were suitable for going out to eat. He basically put himself on house arrest, and it worked. He wrote the book in five and a half months, and he handed it in two weeks early.

Now, in modern society, researchers would refer to that as a "commitment device." And I think commitment devices are powerful, because they can be methods for making habits more attractive. As another example, say that you go to bed tonight and you're thinking to yourself, "All right. Tomorrow's going to be the day. I'm going to wake up and I'm going to go for a run at six." And 6 a.m. rolls around and your bed is warm, it's cold outside and you think, "Maybe I'll just snooze instead."

But if you rewind the clock and go back a day and you text a friend and say, "Hey, let's meet at the park at 6:15 and go for a run," well, now 6 a.m. rolls around, and your bed is still warm, and it's still cold outside, but if you don't get up and go for a run, you're a jerk because you leave your friend at the park all alone. So, suddenly you have simultaneously made the habit of sleeping in less attractive and the habit of getting up and going for a run more attractive.

OK, so you've taken that first step. You're doing the easy entry point, ideally every morning. How do you build from there to more significant, visible progress?

At some point you want to graduate. This is what I call *habit graduation*. You want to step up to the next level. And my general rule of thumb is to try to get 1% better each day. The same way that money multiplies through compound interest, the effects of your habits multiply as you repeat them over time. I like to say habits are the compound interest of self-improvement.

Take reading, for example. Reading one book will not make you a genius. But if you build a habit of reading every day, then not only do you finish one book after another, but with each book you complete, you also have a new frame or a new way to view all the previous books you've read.

And the more connection points you have, the more perspectives you collect . . . that knowledge starts to compound on top of itself. A lot of habits are like that. Take doing an extra 10 minutes of work each day. Maybe that's one more sales call. Maybe it's one more email. Maybe it's just an extra 10 minutes to review the things you've written or revised, or to tweak or improve something.

Doing an extra 10 minutes on one day isn't much. But the difference between someone who doesn't do that and someone who does an extra 10 minutes every day over a 30-year career, that extra time can actually compound to a very surprising degree. That one extra sales call a day can mean a lot over the course of years and decades.

If you have good habits, time becomes your ally. You just need to be patient. You just need to let that compounding process work for you. But if you have bad habits, time becomes your enemy. And each day that clicks by, you dig the hole a little bit deeper, put yourself a little bit farther behind the eight ball.

That does make it sound, though, like it's just linear progression, and you argue very vehemently that it's not. There are going to be times when you stall, times when you regress. You talk about valleys and plateaus. So how do you navigate that emotionally and keep pressing on?

That's a really good point. The emotional part is a really true thing. You hear this a lot. I hear this from my readers a lot. They'll say something like, "I've been running for a month, why can't I see a change in my body?" Or "I've been working on this novel for five and a half months now, the outline's still a mess. Is this thing ever going to be finished?"

When you're in the middle, when you're in the thick of the work, it's really easy to feel that way. And so sometimes I like to equate the process of building your habits to the process of heating up an ice cube. Let's say you walk into a room, and it's cold, like 25 degrees. You can see your breath and there's this ice cube sitting on the table in front of you. And you start to slowly heat the room up, 26, 27, 28 degrees. The ice cube is still sitting there. Then 29, 30, 31, and then you go from 31 to 32 degrees, and it's this one-degree shift that's no different from all the other one-degree shifts that came before it. But suddenly you hit this transition, and the ice cube melts.

The process of building better habits and getting better results is often like that. You're showing up each day, and the degrees are increasing a little bit. You're making these small improvements. You're getting 1% better. But you don't have the outcome that you're trying to achieve. Those delayed rewards haven't showed up yet.

So you feel like giving up, but giving up after doing a habit for a month or three months or six months is kind of like complaining about heating an ice cube from 25 to 31 degrees and it's not melting yet. The work is not being wasted, it's just being stored. And the willingness to stick with it is important.

I really like the San Antonio Spurs. They've won five NBA championships. They've got this quote hanging in their locker room that I think encapsulates this kind of philosophy well. It says something to the effect of, "Whenever I feel like giving up, I think about the stonecutter who takes his hammer and bangs on the rock 100 times without showing a crack. And then at the 101st blow it splits in two. And I know that it wasn't the 101st that did it, but all the 100 that came before."

I think that's exactly the kind of approach to take with your habits. It's not the last sentence that finishes the novel, it's all the ones that came before. It's not the last workout that gives you a fit body, it's all the ones that came before. And if you can be willing to keep showing up and keep hammering on the rock, to keep building up that potential energy, to know that it's not wasted, it's just being stored, then maybe you can start to fight that emotional battle of building better habits and ultimately get to the rewards you're waiting to accumulate.

I know you were an athlete, not a basketball player but a baseball player. Sports is obviously a place where people have to develop good habits and routines. You lift weights every day. You do get stronger over the long term. You hit 100 serves every day, you become more accurate. Even if you plateau or regress, you do sort of see that progress. But it seems much harder in a work context, where the correlation between the effort that you're putting in and then the achievement or reward is less clear.

The key insight here is that you want feedback to be visible and rapid. I think this is so important that in *Atomic Habits* I call it "the cardinal rule of behavior change." Which is this: Behaviors that are immediately rewarded get repeated. Behaviors that are immediately punished get avoided.

In sports, for example, as soon as you hit the serve, you immediately know if it was accurate or not. Is it in or is it out? That rapid feedback allows you to make an adjustment, hopefully a slight one, for the next time. And then you keep repeating that serve. You get this feedback almost instantly.

But in the modern work environment, particularly in large corporations, feedback is very delayed. It's kind of opaque. It's very difficult to see what your contribution is delivering to the bottom line or producing in terms of output.

I think one of the lessons to take away from this is that one of the most motivating feelings for the human brain is a feeling of progress. In the case of your own individual life you can decide what you want to track. This can take multiple forms. For my business, I do a weekly review where each Friday I track key metrics, revenue, expenses, profit, and so on.

My dad likes to swim, for example. Well, any day that he gets out of the pool, his body looks the same when he gets out of the water as it did when he got in. There's no visual feedback. So what he does is take out a little pocket calendar and put an "X" on that day. It's a very minor thing, but it is a signal of progress. It is a signal that he showed up and did the right thing that day.

I think it also reveals a lesson that probably a lot of managers or entrepreneurs can use as well, which is that you want the pace of feedback, the pace of measurement, to match the frequency of the habit.

And what if I have a big goal, like become a better manager? How do I distill that into smaller steps? The kind that you're talking about.

I would start by saying, "OK, I want to be a better manager. Great. That's a good vision. What does a better manager do? What do those daily behaviors look like? What sort of habits does a better manager have? Who is the type of person that could be a better manager?"

Then you start to elicit answers from yourself, such as, "Oh, a better manager gives praise each day." So maybe you build a habit of saying something positive to start off each team meeting. Or, "Oh, a better manager is a role model and models the behavior of the culture. We often talk about transparency, so now I need to build a habit of doing something transparent each day or each week, or in one-on-ones, or whatever. Maybe I start each one-on-one by sharing something about my personal life so that I'm vulnerable first and then my employees follow my lead." You get my point. You start to see which behaviors the identity [of a better manager] is associated with, and then you have something more concrete that you can focus on. You can focus on building those habits rather than being stuck in this high-level meta-mode where you think, "Well, I just really want to be a better manager" but that's very hard to translate into something practical.

So, why is it that good habits seem so hard to form yet easy to break and bad habits seem so easy to form and hard to break?

I thought about this a lot when I was working on *Atomic Habits* because I think, actually, asking that question can reveal a lot about what we want to do to build a good habit or to break a bad one.

Let's say we want to build good habits. Well, how come bad habits stick so readily? What you find is that they have a variety of qualities. The first quality that bad habits often have is that they're very obvious. For example, let's say that eating at fast-food restaurants is a bad habit or a habit that you don't want to perform as much.

Well, in America it's hard to drive down the street for more than 15 minutes without passing at least a few, if not a dozen, fast-food restaurants. They're very obvious. They're very prevalent in the environment. So that's a lesson that we can take and apply to our good habits. If you want a good habit to stick, then you should make it a big part of your environment.

Another quality that bad habits often have is that they're incredibly convenient. They're very frictionless. The incredible convenience of many bad habits is a big reason why we stick to them so much. So if you want your good habits to stick, they need to be as easy and convenient as possible.

Another quality of bad habits is that the benefit is usually immediate and the cost is usually delayed. And with good habits it's often the reverse. So the benefit of going to the gym for a week is not a whole lot. If anything, your body's sore. You haven't really changed. You look the same in the mirror. The scale is roughly the same. It's only if you stick to that habit for a year or two or three that you get the outcome you want.

So there's this gap. There's sort of this valley of death in the beginning with a lot of good habits. You start doing them, but you don't have the immediate rewards that you're showing up and hoping you get. Whereas with bad habits there's this mismatch between the immediate outcome that you get ("Hey this feels great in the moment, I should do this") and then it turns out that it ultimately hurts you in the long run.

The cost of your good habits is in the present. The cost of your bad habits is in the future. A lot of the reason why bad habits form so readily and good habits are so unlikely, or resistant to form, has to do with that gap in time and reward.

Originally published December 31, 2019. HBR IdeaCast episode 716

About the Contributors

TERESA M. AMABILE is the Edsel Bryant Ford Professor of Business Administration at Harvard Business School. She researches what makes people creative, productive, happy, and motivated at work. She is a coauthor of *The Progress Principle* (HBR Press, 2011).

ALISON BEARD is a senior editor at *Harvard Business Review*.

JULIAN BIRKINSHAW is a professor at London Business School. His most recent book is *Fast/Forward: Make Your Company Fit for the Future*.

RICHARD BOYATZIS is a professor in the Departments of Organizational Behavior, Psychology, and Cognitive Science at the Weatherhead School of Management and Distinguished University Professor at Case Western Reserve University. He is a cofounder of the Coaching Research Lab and coauthor of *Helping People Change* (HBR Press, 2019).

BRIANNA BARKER CAZA is an associate professor of management in the Bryan School of Business and Economics at the University of North Carolina at Greensboro.

JAMES CLEAR is a writer and speaker. He is the author of the bestselling book *Atomic Habits*.

JORDAN COHEN is the vice president of talent development, learning and enablement at MediaMath. He also serves as an adviser to the management training firm LifeLabs Learning.

EDWARD T. COKELY is a professor of psychology at the University of Oklahoma and is cofounding faculty of the National Institute for Risk & Resilience.

JAY A. CONGER is the Henry R. Kravis Research Professor in Leadership Studies at Claremont McKenna College. He is the coauthor of the book *The High Potential's Advantage* (HBR Press, 2018).

PETER F. DRUCKER was an Austrian-born American management consultant, educator, and author whose writings contributed to the philosophical and practical foundations of the modern business corporation. He was also a leader in the development of management education; he invented the concept known as management by objectives; and he has been described as "the founder of modern management."

JANE DUTTON is the Robert L. Kahn Distinguished University Professor of Business Administration and Psychology at the University of Michigan's Ross School of Business. She is cofounder of the Center for Positive Organizations at Ross.

SCOTT K. EDINGER, founder of Edinger Consulting, is a coauthor of *The Hidden Leader* and *The Butterfly Effect*. Follow Scott on Twitter @ScottKEdinger or on LinkedIn.

K. ANDERS ERICSSON was a Swedish psychologist and Conradi Eminent Scholar and Professor of Psychology at Florida State University. He was internationally recognized as a researcher in the psychological nature of expertise and human performance.

SYDNEY FINKELSTEIN is the Steven Roth Professor of Management at the Tuck School of Business at Dartmouth College, the author of *The Superbosses Playbook*, and the host of *The Sydcast* podcast. Connect with him on Twitter @sydfinkelstein.

JOSEPH R. FOLKMAN is the president of Zenger Folkman, a leadership development consultancy. He is a coauthor of the book *The New Extraordinary Leader*. Connect with Joe on Twitter @joefolkman.

DANIEL GOLEMAN, best known for his writing on emotional intelligence, is codirector of the Consortium for Research on Emotional Intelligence in Organizations at Rutgers University. His latest book is *Building Blocks of Emotional Intelligence*, a 12-primer set on each of the emotional intelligence competencies, and he offers training on the competencies through an online learning platform, Emotional Intelligence Training Programs. His other books include *Primal Leadership* and *Altered Traits*.

HEIDI GRANT is a social psychologist who researches, writes, and speaks about the science of motivation. She is director of learning research and development for EY Americas. Her most recent book is *Reinforcements*. She's also the author of *Nine Things Successful People Do Differently* and *No One Understands You and What to Do About It*.

EMILY HEAPHY is an assistant professor of management at the Isenberg School of Management at the University of Massachusetts Amherst.

LINDA A. HILL is the Wallace Brett Donham Professor of Business Administration at Harvard Business School. She is the author of *Becoming a Manager* and a coauthor of *Being the Boss* and *Collective Genius*.

STEVEN J. KRAMER is a psychologist and independent researcher. He is a coauthor of *The Progress Principle* (HBR Press, 2011).

ELLEN LANGER is a professor of psychology at Harvard University and founder of the Langer Mindfulness Institute. She has been described as the "mother of mindfulness" and is a recipient of a Guggenheim Fellowship and three Distinguished Scientist Awards, the World Congress Award, the NYU Alumni Achievement Award, and the Staats Award for Unifying Psychology.

ANNIE McKEE is a senior fellow at the University of Pennsylvania Graduate School of Education and the director of the Penn CLO Executive Doctoral Program. She is the author of *How to Be Happy at Work* and a coauthor of *Primal Leadership, Resonant Leadership,* and *Becoming a Resonant Leader*.

MICHAEL J. PRIETULA is a professor at the Goizueta Business School at Emory University and a visiting research scholar at the Institute for Human and Machine Cognition in Pensacola, Florida.

ROBERT QUINN is a professor emeritus at the University of Michigan's Ross School of Business and a cofounder of the school's Center for Positive Organizations.

DOUGLAS A. READY is a senior lecturer at MIT's Sloan School of Management and the founder and president of ICEDR.

LAURA MORGAN ROBERTS is a professor of practice at the University of Virginia's Darden School of Business, and the coeditor of *Race, Work, and Leadership: New Perspectives on the Black Experience* (HBR Press, 2019).

GRETCHEN SPREITZER is the Keith E. and Valerie J. Alessi Professor of Business Administration at the University of Michigan's Ross School of Business, where she is a core faculty member in the Center for Positive Organizations.

JOHN H. ZENGER is the CEO of Zenger Folkman, a leadership development consultancy. He is a coauthor of *The New Extraordinary*. Connect with Jack on Twitter @jhzenger.

Index

Engage with HBR content the way you want, on any device.

With HBR's subscription plans, you can access world-renowned case studies from Harvard Business School and receive four **free eBooks**. Download and customize prebuilt **slide decks and graphics** from our **Data & Visuals** collection. With HBR's archive, top 50 best-selling articles, and five new articles every day, HBR is more than just a magazine.

Subscribe Today
HBR.org/success

Harvard
Business
Review